To
Bill Lacy

*

ganz herzlich
your A. Achtimes

*

Chicago
30
VI
96

Andrea Mesecke / Thorsten Scheer

Museum of Contemporary Art Chicago
Josef Paul Kleihues

with a foreword by
Udo Kultermann

photographs by
Hélène Binet

Gebr. Mann Verlag • Berlin

Imprint
Layout, Cover: Thorsten Scheer, Essen
Setting, Design:
Axel Schuch (Kontrast Studios), Bochum
Translation (foreword excepted):
Michael Robinson, London
Repro and Production: NovaConcept, Berlin
Printed by: DruckConcept, Berlin
Photography: Hélène Binet, London

ISBN 3–7861–1436–6

The authors thank the employees of the Harold
Washington Library Center, Visual and Performing
Arts Division (especially Angie Holtzmann), the
employees of the Chicago Historical Society Prints
and Photographs Department (especially Eileen
Flanagan) and Library, Johannes Rath, project man-
ager in Kleihues's Chicago office, and Helmut
Geisert, publisher's editor. Our special thanks go
to Josef P. Kleihues and the Director of the MCA
Kevin E. Consey.

Contents

Udo Kultermann

Merging Tradition and the Consciousness of Crisis
The Museum of Contemporary Art in Chicago

The history of the building type museum is short in comparison with other building types, but since the 18th century it has a series of distinguished manifestations which contributed to the changing needs of each new period. The new Museum of Contemporary Art in Chicago by Josef P. Kleihues adds another dimension to its history, both in regard to the specific features of the type and to how it functions in the context of the city.[1]

From its early beginnings the museum as a building type has gone through important social and political transformations. It grew according to the necessity of relating a contemporary consciousness to tradition, in other words, to harmonize the continuity of cultural experience in an institution that programmatically transcended the feudalistic power structure of the old monarchies. Hegel's dictum – often misunderstood – that "art in its highest sense is and must remain a thing of the past", has to be seen as the crucial point at which time art and art history began to coexist. At the same time Goethe defined the museum as "an infinite in movement" (ein Unendliches in Bewegung).[2]

The formation of the museum as an institution of society is the most visible manifestation of this historical transformation. It produced brilliant architectural solutions by architects such as Schinkel, Klenze and Semper, which became dominating building types of the period.

The development into the 20th century continued with further adaptations of the established building type, according to the changing conditions of what a museum was considered to be and where in the social and urban context it should be located. Since its early inception museums have contained a wide range of material, from historical artifacts to scientific models, works of art and collectible objects. Architecturally, the most significant manifestations of museums buildings remained devoted to the art of the past and historic documents.[3]

A specific new type of museum emerged when society demanded that works by contemporary artists also be given a space for permanent display. This required a new emphasis to align the building type with the changing tendencies of the contemporary art developments. Alfred Barr's Museum of Modern

7

Art in New York by Godwin and Stone was of programmatic importance in this context, and it inaugurated a large number of museums buildings in which the production of art and its preserving spacial configurations entered a new symbiosis.[4]

More than the former manifestations of museums buildings in general, the new type of museum of contemporary art had a unique character. In each case the problem had to be solved as to how the building will serve the unique type of collection, whether tailored to its permanent and unchangeable display, or as a flexible open-ended space in which different types of work can be exhibited. Victoria Newhouse asked in 1995: "Should museums architecture be a background or a foreground for its content?"[5]

The debate between artists and architects in regard to the relationship between the significance of the building type and the way to exhibit the art has a long history, and arguments on both sides have been intensely exchanged. One artist is Markus Lüpertz, who advocated against the architects: "This trend, killing architecture with art or, vice versa, architecture's attempt to be more than art, is the problem facing us today".[6] There have been other arguments suggesting dissolving the museum in favor of a greater integration of works of art into the public context.

Josef P. Kleihues is in favor of the museum as an institution which has a place in society. He firmly believes that there is a legitimate need to display works of art in an institution which should be different from a department store or a warehouse.[7] The Museum of Contemporary Art in Chicago is thus a realistic approach to bring harmony to the varying, often contradicting, demands a museums architect has to face. In an interview Josef P. Kleihues expressed his intentions "to create exhibition space where nothing should excite you except the art".[8] And the present director of the museum, Kevin E. Consey, has echoed these convictions: "We exhibit, collect, interpret, and preserve contemporary art, in a manner that I think is akin to journalism. We try to make sense of art history as it's unfolding." And he added: "That process is necessarily messy, difficult, even confrontational. It can be unsettling for our visitors, in much the same way that a morning newspaper is unsettling. But it should also excite and enliven and engage".[9]

It ist significant that both, the architect and the director of the Museum of Contemporary Art in Chicago, used the term 'excite' in their statements as it is this particular term that is often missing in the tradial vocabulary of museums. The excitement in experiencing contemporary works of art in all their endless and contradicting manifestations are crucial elements for the present situation as well as the state of crisis in contemporary art and architecture.[10]

Josef P. Kleihues used a similar realistic approach when he explained his function as the director of the International Building Exhibition in Berlin some years ago: "I was concerned to find an approach that, instead of striving for a higher unity based on the dissolution of different or conflicting interests, would aim at solving a merely apparent contradiction, by encouraging the free, and in a sense even autonomous development of the separate elements of the city (building, block, street, square) while ensuring their integration into a larger whole, an order made recognizable by the history of the city and its genius loci".[11]

It is significant that one of the most relevant characteristics of the new Museum of Contemporary Art in Chicago is its integration into an urban and historical context in which it not only respects the physical environment of the city of Chicago, but also the cultural tradition of Chicago Pragmatism. The architectural tradition of the School of Chicago, including Henry Hobson Richardson, Le Baron Jenney, Louis Sullivan and John Wellborn Root even influenced some of the architectural details in the new museum building.[12] As a result, in the design of an architect from Berlin the cross-cultural relations between the German Classicism of Schinkel and his American followers as well as the reverberations of Hegelian philosophy in American Pragmatism are newly emphazised.[13]

Both architectural form and location of the building reflect the wish to make it part of the cultural reality of Chicago. The building block, on the site of a former Armory demolished in 1993, has an open view to Lake Michigan and is part of an urban green belt. Located between two public parks the site is a kind of urban canyon with the sculpture garden of the museum as a part of the larger city park system.[14]

The architectural and urban concept of Josef P. Kleihues is not oriented on devices which require historical quotations nor does it follow the doctrin

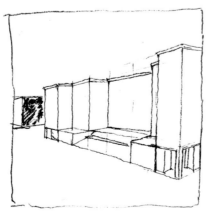

of a rigid modernity. Instead, it accepts the specific situation of the site, its cultural and architectural tradition and the general requirements of a pragmatic solution for a museum of contemporary art in the center of a large city. It demonstates the ambitions of an architect who earlier had defined his version of modernity in this way: "Modernity, defined as a vital awareness of history and a vitalizing awareness of crisis, can never be as clear-cut or absolute as the classical modern architects still thought it could be. Modernity today is a consciousness of crisis, existential, lived through."[15]

1 About the formation of the building type museum: Francis Henry Taylor, Babel's Tower, New York 1945; Francis Henry Taylor, The Taste of Angels: A History of Collecting from Ramses to Napoleon, Boston 1948; Udo Kultermann, "Das Museum - gestern - heute - morgen", Die Innenarchitektur 3 (1958); Michael Brawne, The New Art Museums, New York 1965; Helmut Seling, "The Genesis of the Museum", Architectural Review (February 1967); Alma S. Witlin, Museums. In Search of a Usable Past, Cambridge (MA) 1970.

2 Udo Kultermann, The History of Art History, New York 1993, pp. 61 ff.; the quote by Goethe after: Udo Kultermann, "Vom Rittergut zum Kunstmuseum. Schloß Morsbroich. Ein Weg durch sieben Jahrhunderte", Artis 3 (1967).

3 Among the most significant art museums in recent decades are buildings by Frank Lloyd Wright, Ludwig Mies van der Rohe, Le Corbusier, Louis I. Kahn, James Stirling, Gottfried Böhm, Hans Hollein, Frank O. Gehry and Tadao Ando.

4 A. H. Barr, "Modern Art Makes History, Too", College Art Journal (November 1941); A. H. Barr, Painting and Sculpture in the Museum of Modern Art, New York 1948; Alice Goldfarb Marquis, A. H. Barr, Jr.: Missionar for the Modern, Chicago 1989.

5 Victoria Newhouse, "New Museums Stimulate New Art", Architecture (December 1995); see also Herbert Read, "The Museum and the Artist", College Art Journal (Summer 1954); André Malraux, Museum Without Walls, London 1967; Maurice Tuchman and others, "Validating Modern Art: The Impact of the Museums on Modern Art History", Artforum (January 1977); E. H. Gombrich, "The Museum. Past, Present and Future", Critical Inquiry (Spring 1977); Josef P. Kleihues, The Museum Projects. Edited by Kim Shkapich, New York 1989.

6 Markus Lüpertz, "Art and Architecture", New Museum Buildings in the Federal Republic of Germany. Edited by Heinrich Klotz and Waltraud Krase, Frankfurt/M. 1985, p. 32; about other contributions to the ongoing discussion see also Udo Kultermann, "Das Museum ist noch zu retten", Junge Stimme (January 23, 1965); Daniel Buren, "Function of the Museum", Artforum (September 1973); Hans Haacke, "Museums: Manager of Consciousness" Art in America (February 1984); Douglas Crimp, "The Postmodern Museum", Parachute 46 (1987); "The End of Art and the Origin of the Museum", The Art Quarterly (Winter 1987); Douglas Crimp, On the Museum's Ruins, Cambridge (MA) 1993; W. Hofmann, "Das Kunstmuseum - Kirche und/ oder Warenhaus", Neues Museum. Die österreichische Museumszeitschrift 3/4 (1994).

7 Unpublished interview (1996).

8 Unpublished interview (1996).

9 Unpublished interview (1996).

10 Since its foundation in 1967 the collection of the museum has grown rapidly and today includes, among many other works, major paintings by artists such as René Magritte, Francis Bacon, Barnett Newman, Ad Reinhardt, Lucio Fontana, Franz Kline, Andy Warhol, Joseph Beuys, Anselm Kiefer, Malcolm Morley, Bruce Neuman and Ana Mendieta. The concept of the museum is not limited to painting and sculpture, but programmatically also includes video art, performance art and other recent disciplines.

11 Josef P. Kleihues, "From the Destruction to the Critical Reconstruction of the City: Urban Design in Berlin After 1945", Berlin – New York. Like and Unlike. Essays on Architecture and Art from 1870 to the Present. Edited by Josef P. Kleihues and Christine Rathgeber, New York 1993, p. 407.

12 About the School of Chicago see Carl W. Condit, The Chicago School of Architecture, Chicago 1964.

13 See the essays by Andrea Mesecke and Thorsten Scheer in this volume; about Peirce: Charles Sanders Peirce, Schriften I. Zur Entstehung des Pragmatismus. Edited by Karl-Otto Apel, Frankfurt/M. 1967; about Dewey: Udo Kultermann, "John Dewey's 'Art as Experience': A Reevaluation of Aesthetic Pragmatism", art and criticism 3 (1990); Udo Kultermann, "'Kunst als Erlebnis'. John Dewey", Kunst und Wirklichkeit. Von Fiedler bis Derrida. Zehn Annäherungen, Munich 1991, p. 131 ff.

14 A. E. Brinckmann, Stadtbaukunst. Geschichtliche Querschnitte und neuzeitliche Ziele, Berlin 1920; Paul Gilbert and Charles Lee Bryson, Chicago and Its Makers, Chicago 1929.

15 Kleihues 1993, loc. cit., p. 407.

Collage using an aerial
photograph showing the
new MCA site between
Michigan Avenue and
Lake Michigan. Even in
his first sketches J. P.
Kleihues had proposed
bridging Lake Shore
Drive to create a direct
link between the lake
and the city, which was
to be extended parallel
with the busy road as a
pedestrian promenade.

"The most important centres of the urban
community can be grasped from the Propylaea
at a single glance."
Sigfried Giedion, 1969¹

Old World – New World

Josef P. Kleihues's Museum of Contemporary
Art Chicago is an architectural complex that
reflects the history of the city of Chicago, its building
traditions and its manifold relations with Europe in
a number of ways.

The rules of the chessboard-like ground plan, also a
characteristic feature of Chicago, were formulated
by Hippodamus as early as the 5th century BC.
When the port of Miletus on the west coast of Asia
Minor was founded in 479 BC it was above all the
democratic and egalitarian basic idea that played a
decisive role in shaping the grid plan, along with the
functional quality of the ordering structure. The dimensions of the rectangular blocks, at that time related to the size of single-family houses, were adapt-
ed to changing requirements right down to the
modern industrial city in the 19th century. The right-
angled ground plan was particularly highly es-
teemed as an ideal concept in the Renaissance. In
the 16th century it spread to South and Central
America as a result of Spanish conquests (Caracas/
Venezuela founded in 1567), and as their power base
extended northwards into the present United States
(Savannah/Georgia founded around 1733). Thomas
Jefferson systematized the historic process in 1785
by relating it to degrees of latitude and longitude.
The method was then applied to the colonization of
the North American West, and is still in existence
today.

Chicago acquired its right-angled grid from James
Thompson when the city was founded in 1830. The
greatest possible economic – and therefore architectural – exploitation of the blocks was to be seen in
the historic city centre, later the Loop, even before
the fire in 1871; this also set the pattern for other districts as part of the intense concentration of economic forces after the disaster. The city grew explo-
sively, leading to enormous increases in height and
almost complete coverage of the plot areas. The
street corridor with its closed building line became
the predominant urban development element. In
order to give the buildings a certain architectural ex-
pressiveness even though block-edge development
meant that they could not be fully formulated sculp-
turally, architects from then on concentrated on ornamental treatment for building surfaces; this is
crucially significant for any aesthetic assessment of
the Chicago School of Architecture.

The MCA building plot is between East Chicago Avenue and Pearson Street. In his first design, Josef P. Kleihues related to historical development and planned to close the edge of the rectangular site with two sections in the form of adjacent squares, linked with the Lake Shore Playground on the eastern side. The western border of the plot is Mies van

der Rohe Way – formerly Seneca Street, and recently renamed after the famous German-American architect as he lived in the neighbouring corner building in Pearson Street/Mies van der Rohe Way for many years. The entrance to the new museum building is here; this rises above the first square, while the square to the east is occupied by a sculpture garden. It is appropriate to Josef P. Kleihues's rationalist design methods that he uses a uniform building grid as his base and relates all dimensions to this. This is also guaranteed in principle in the Museum of Contemporary Art. The building grid is illustrated in the wall zone by continuous bands to the breadth of a basic 2-foot module, and also in the dimensions of

the square slabs in the base area. However, if the base grid is compared with the wall zone structure, one detects a geometrical shift that is not typical of Kleihues's architecture. Under ideal circumstances all the dimensions of the building should go into each other equally. However, this shift was produced by a change in the building's dimensions that occurred because Kleihues was compelled to revise the design in a second phase for cost reasons. Instead of the 198 x 198 feet of the first design (7 axes of 28 feet = 196 feet plus one foot on each side to complete the basic module at the edges of the building), Kleihues decided in a remarkably pragmatic way simply to reduce the dimensions of the building, so that it was ultimately realized on the scale of 184 x 184 feet (7 axes of 26 feet = 182 feet plus one foot on each side to complete the basic module at the edges of the building). But keeping the 2-foot basic module means that the façade units measuring 26 feet di-

vide up into odd numbers, unlike the first design.[2] Kleihues persuaded himself to retain and accept the contradiction because he had come to terms with the pragmatism of American culture, but the revelation of the resulting geometrical conflict agrees with his theoretical position, which is based on logical transparency and argumentative clarity.

The horizontal articulation of the building follows classical tectonics with its division into base, wall zone and cornice. The base is clad in light yellow limestone, and above it is the wall zone, pierced by a very few windows, with delicately structured aluminium sheets in front of them. It feels permissible to remember Frank Lloyd Wright's 1892 Charnley House in north Chicago for the Adler and Sullivan office. The use of light sandstone for the base, along with the two-dimensional wall treatment, is only the most obvious correspondence with the museum building. The tectonic construction and structure of Charnley House make it a residential building that links up with European culture, similar in interpretation to Karl Friedrich Schinkel's model design for rented accommodation, for example.[3] Here too the body of the building is broken up in the zone above the ground floor, as is also the case in Charnley House, in the form of a broad projecting bay window above the central entrance area with a set-back attic storey in the central zone.

Kleihues varies the motif by taking account of the modern structural principles of skeleton building. The side entrances to the building at ground level – on the left ground-level access suitable for the handicapped and on the right the entrance to the bookshop – are negative cuts out of the stereometric

Frank Lloyd Wright, Charnley House, 1892.

Karl Friedrich Schinkel, model design for rented accommodation, 1826.

Museum of Contemporary Art, perspective view with corner support (screen print).

body of the building. The outer edge of the building is traced at this point by a support that also reproduces the structure of the grid. The rational system contradicts the relationship of bearing and load anticipated when looking at the building in terms of the slender dimensions of the supports, but Kleihues can afford to ignore this as the rational system agrees with the actual conditions, in other words the actual functioning of the structure.

On the same side of the building in Mies van der Rohe Way the reduced building volume made it possible to construct an extension in the form of an urban square, clearly related to the articulation of the building and integral to the overall conception as a result of the structure of its stone covering.

The visitor is brought to the building by a flight of steps 78 feet wide framed on both sides. The staircase refers in terms of motif to eminent models in architectural history, starting originally with the access to the ancient Acropolis in Athens, the, and conveyed above all in the reception of Karl Friedrich Schinkel in Berlin building history.

Julien-David Le Roy, in his book "Les ruines des plus beaux monuments de la Grèce", 1758, was the first to publish reconstructed illustrations of the Propylaea, important parts of which had already been destroyed by this time. The lack of precision in these illustrations was violently criticized at the time by English contemporaries, who had visited Athens before Le Roy, but did not publish their discoveries until seven years later. They unleashed a long-lasting academic argument about the original condition, which incidentally was never about the side

framing of the steps, but was concerned above all with the symmetrical arrangement of the parts of the building and the pedestals in front, to which Kleihues – as it were following an interpretation that was idealized in this sense – also refers with the sculpture pedestals on either side of the steps. One important result of Le Roy's interpretation, disregarding the lack of precision in the details, was the tradition of depicting the building symmetrically, which continued to be the case in literature on the subject. Le Roy based himself on a textual description of ancient origin and made the building symmetrical in his perspective illustration, with two flanking wings in each case and sculpture pedestals in front.

The 1758 publication may have expressed an additional possibility of doubt in its hatched depiction of the side that had been assumed to exist previously, but by the time of Durand's 1799–1801 representa-

tion uncertainty had given way to 18th century interests. It was no longer possible to imagine an admirable building that was not based on symmetry and regularity. Carl Gotthard Langhans's Brandenburg Gate, built as an entrance to Berlin, was also driven by a wish for unity and is therefore constructed in strict symmetry. In this context Schinkel's 1834 plan for a King's Square on the Acropolis is of interest. Schinkel's knowledge of Greece was drawn from sources available to him in print; he had never been there himself. He clearly relied on Jacques-Guillaume Legrand's 1806 work "Galerie antique", which was available to him before Eduard Schaubert and Christian Hansen's "Die Akropolis von Athen" appeared in Berlin in 1839. In his design the right wing of the Propylaea, apart from a pathway through on the right-hand side, is represented strictly symmetrically, appropriately to his age's need for symmetry, although Schinkel did draw attention to "a misunderstanding in the concept of symmetry, which had brought about so much hypocrisy and boredom ...", when writing about the structure of the palace concerned in a letter accompanying the design[4] to his client, the Crown Prince of Bavaria.

He drew the staircase with an intermediate landing that corresponds with no known reconstruction attempt and must therefore be considered as Schinkel's addition. The same is true of the trapezoid extension of the staircase towards the right-hand side, which Schinkel gained by reflecting the axis provided by the surviving statue plinth on the left. The extended staircase ends before the victory temple, to avoid conflict with this building.

Although the traditional reconstruction of the Propylaea in a spirit of symmetry was disturbed by more precise building requirements in the first half of the nineteenth century, Kleihues is definitely relating to the interpretation of the theme as conveyed by its Berlin reception. Only this guarantees a memory of the traditions intended: Greece and Berlin.

In 1863 Louis-François-Philippe Boitte, in "Envoi de Rome", spoke of balance and equilibrium of masses rather than symmetry, and the important interpretation by Auguste Choisy in his 1899 "Histoire de l'architecture", which was valid for a long time, expressed a view that had now completely detached itself from the idealism of the neoclassical ethic.

Schinkel's Schauspielhaus in the Gendarmenmarkt (1818-1821) still clearly relates to the idealized interpretation of classicism, even though its use of the motif relates above all to the steps and adjacent portico. The Museum in the Lustgarten, dating from 1822-1828, one of the first public museums anywhere, relates to this motif with its steps. The Schauspielhaus may owe a very great deal to the literal classicism indicated, but Schinkel's design for the museum already shows an approach influenced by Romanticism, which questions the architectural elements used in terms of their effect, then applies them appropriately. The Schauspielhaus expresses itself in a way that is completely appropriate to the classical building tradition in terms of proportions, the number of columns used and the crowning tympanum. The museum, however, has Ionic columns that are also appropriate to the aesthetics of antiquity, but their monotactic run of 18 columns scarcely manages to convey the impression of a temple façade. In the access area to the museum at the top of the steps another row of columns is added on the level of the concluding lateral outer walls. This creates a transitional area, which articulates the mediation of internal and external space, in the spirit of opening up the building conceptually to the citizens of Berlin. The interior central rotunda, unlike the other sections, relates to Roman antiquity, especially the Pantheon in Rome, and indicates that Schinkel was prepared to use entirely contradictory formal ideas in the service of a particular effect, as was appropriate to the stylistic pluralism of his later work.

This motif, perceived in Greek antiquity as a transitional zone to the mythological and religious temple precinct, is reinterpreted even as early as Schinkel to perform the public function of giving access to cultural institutions that were new at that time. Kleihues makes this motif and its reception part of his design concept and enhances it in the spirit of a contemporary building task. It seems quite natural to use steps placed at the side of a museum building, but here various aspects are added which make

Karl Friedrich Schinkel, Museum in the Lustgarten, 1822-1828.

Kleihues's thinking both comprehensible and open to experience. He further works against the monumentalization of the traditional motif – already relativized by Schinkel in the Lustgarten Museum – intending to democratize it by his conscious violation of classical aesthetic conventions.

Classical architecture's idea of harmony was based on arranging façade units in even numbers, so that the axis of symmetry lay between the supports or wall surfaces. But Kleihues's design uses a *fausse axe* produced by grouping six window axes on the façade of the core structure and, in contrast with the classical division, creating an impression of a rather more serial accumulation of units of the same shape. Here Kleihues confronts the knowing reminiscence of the classical motif with a fundamental infringement of the rules, which means that symmetry does not appear as a total ordering principle of

Museum of Contemporary Art, entrance façade.

conventional aesthetics but acquires its meaning from relativization of the remembered historical motif. The core area of the building, open to the inside because it is fully glazed, additionally reinforces the inviting effect that emanates from the steps themselves.

In the first design this glazed core area rising through the full height of the building was still a pure glass façade, while now it emphasizes the articulating elements of the rest of the façade by means of continuous window bands, thus illustrating its systematic nature.

The entrance hall that opens up behind the glass wall is distinguished by its breadth and generosity. The bright space, full of vistas and defined exclusively by windows or white walls, is open on all sides, thus contrasting with the closed appearance of the exterior. Visitors can get their bearings here, and have the choice of setting off in various directions. They are to a certain extent emancipated from being guided by the architecture in that the space offers a large number of directions without especially accentuating any of them. At the same time the interior space extends over the width of the glazed façade into the side wings on both sides, and is open above through all the floors. This creates a spatial experience that makes the viewer sense that the interior of the building is larger than the external form suggests. The motif of a covering and its development into the interior, to use Kleihues's words, finds visible expression here.

An open view straight ahead takes visitors through the building to the glazed façade at the back, enabling them to look out over the sculpture garden into the city and Lake Michigan, where the view fades on the horizon of the sheet of water.

The motif of the old world, the memory of the tradition of Greek antiquity, is quoted by Kleihues on the basis of its architectural tradition, Schinkel's Berlin buildings, and articulated in order to open up the building. The fact that the motif is turned into a symbol here clearly serves to invite the observer, and not for reasons of monumentalization. The referential character of the steps is to be understood as congruent to the definition of borders by the glazed façade. Columns would have had to come after the top of the steps to conform with the typology, but in Kleihues's museum the glazed core area of the museum appears instead, rising through a storey. The stylization of the starting motif, the Propylaea, by means of the actual symbolization of the border function and the simultaneous visual dissolution of this border, presents itself as post-modern in the best sense of the concept as it is critically understood. The building relates to the adjacent sculpture garden in terms of the artistic procedure that Kleihues calls *coincidentia oppositorum*, to which he relates through the concept of Poetic Rationalism. Jointly inscribed into the form of the site's double square, the rational structure of the building is here confronted with the comparatively freely – poetically – designed garden. This poeticization of the aesthetic experience, illustrated in the visitor's path and view, makes the city space open to experience by the visitor beyond the actually designed architectural stock by the reception range the building offers. The view, dissolving in the distance of the lake, transcends a natural space experienced as separate from the ordering architectural structure and may appear as a reminiscence of the sublime as a result of the poetic motif, in the spirit of the English scholar Edmund Burke (1729-1797), who was important to the German Enlightenment.

Museum of Contemporary Art, view from the gallery to Lake Michigan.

1   Architektur und das Phänomen des Wandels, Tübingen 1969, p. 18.
2   See explanatory text on "Geometry and Dimensions" in the building documentation.
3   Sammlung architektonischer Entwürfe, Berlin 1819-1840, no. 10, 1826, sheet 67.
4   For the contents of this letter see: Wolzogen, Schinkel's Nachlaß, vol. 3, pp. 333-335.
5   For this question see: Jacques Lucan, "The Propylaion of the Acropolis in Athens: an Architectural Mystery", Daidalos 15 (March 1985), pp. 42-56.

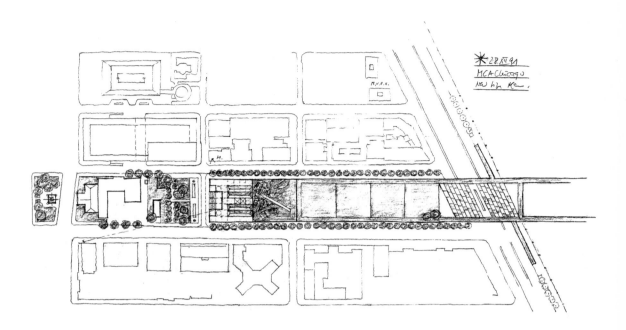

*28 XII 91
MCA Chicago
New h.h. Ka.

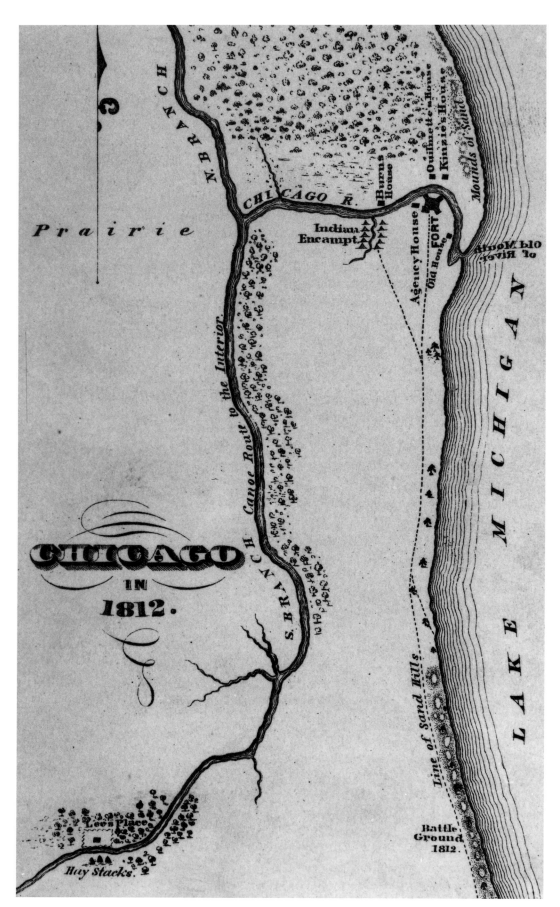

Chicago in 1812 with
the first Fort Dearborn
and an Indian Settle-
ment.

A Place in its Time

Thanks to more recent ways of looking at things, the idea that America has no architecture of its own, and absolutely no modern architecture of its own, as this was imported from Europe with the "International Style", is finally breaking down. The American art historian Lewis Mumford explains the previously excessive reverence for the "International Style" by the fact that many Americans have no self-confidence when faced with their country's supposed lack of history and tradition.[1] Today we can see that so-called classical Modernism did involve rigorous rejection of the historical substance of European "reminiscence architecture", but was not an unrelated phenomenon that had suddenly appeared. To this extent it makes sense that the universality of the imported "International Style" was first perceived as a suitable identification element for the young, democratically structured American nation. But now that classical Modernism has itself become historical and given way to revised Modernism it should be seen in the context of its development history – in Europe and America.

Modern American architecture, today present all over the world, is part of a many-faceted movement that pays as much attention to tradition, climatic conditions and customary local materials as the multiplicity of modern possibilities and the individuality of the landscape or urban context. It is the architect's unique powers of imagination and his expressive will that interprets what is usual, self-repeating, exchangeable and unified from a personal point of view and expresses it in a new way. But the history of architecture does not consist only of individual pioneering achievements. Intellectual exchange in an open society tirelessly fertilizes and enriches the creative dynamics of the common development of our civilization and thus prevents it from ossifying into convention.

What would the influential Chicago School of Architecture be without Louis Sullivan? And what would Louis Sullivan be without French philosophical positivism and the British Arts and Crafts movement? And, conversely, what would European Modernism be without Frank Lloyd Wright, Sullivan's famous pupil from Wisconsin? Frank Lloyd Wright took the open ground plan of rural American architecture seriously in its significance for private living habits and made this fact architecturally visible on the outside. He took the traditional legacy as a reason for creative analysis of new technical possibilities and created an up-to-date, vital synthesis of tradition, machine aesthetics and structural economic viability. But what is American about America? What does a European architect coming to America address? What is he confronted with, what contribution can he make, and what does he take back with him? America was still a long way away from most European achievements less than 200 years ago, but could counter with many pleasant features that had long since been sacrificed to civilizing development in the old world. At that time Europe's cultural discomfort drew the envious eyes of romantics across the ocean to that happy country that had never known feudalism and was considered an incarnation of the "Declaration of Independence". The idea of Utopia realized determined the European view of

America in the 19th century and well into the 20th century. America gave Europe hope, but there was also a growing sense of distaste for the young nation whose citizens abandoned European values and worked hard and successfully towards their common goal of being free and independent. Without the fetters of inherited social structures and the burden of cultural tradition, America successfully went along the road of finding solutions to problems that had defeated the old world. American philosophy and American architecture, which both developed in the last third of the 19th century, are two examples of a developing new tradition that arose from an impressive coming to terms with the industrial age and brought the nation's independent identity to maturity. Superior American development on the basis of egalitarian democratic principles was

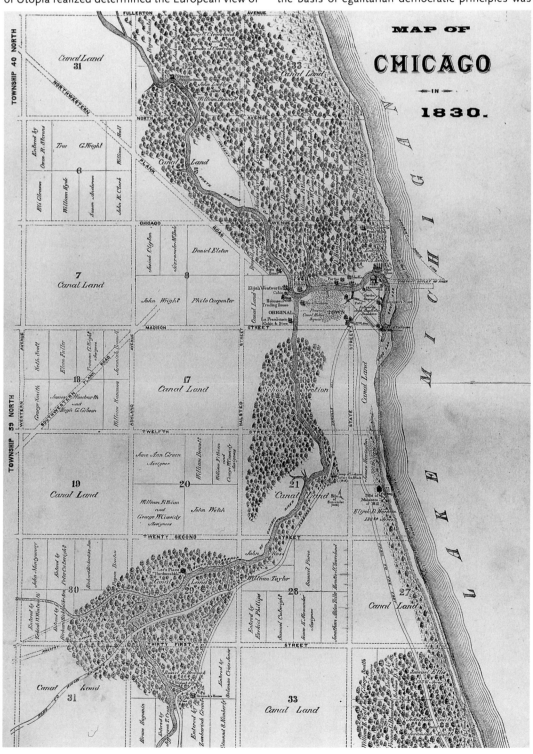

First land distribution in Chicago c. 1830.

also enthusiastically celebrated in Europe after the turn of the century. The fact that opportunity about progress contributed to a transfiguration of reality on both sides is only one expression of the apparently insuperable discrepancy between theory and practice.

Bertrand Russell felt that America did the best work in the field of philosophy and psychology in this century. Not so much because of individual talents, but because they were independent of certain traditions that European thinkers had inherited from Middle Ages. Where intellectual America managed to shake off the fetters of Europe, it became free to take a new view, thanks above all to James and Dewey.[2] Here Russell is talking about American pragmatism, which was first introduced to the philosophers named in the early 20th century, after Charles Sanders Peirce had defined the concept 30 years before.

Pragmatism: from Philosophy to Weltanschauung

In everyday use, pragmatism is associated with an American *Weltanschauung*, linked with the idea that action expresses a person's nature and is superior to thought. This simplification was caused by imprecise formulations by the inventor, Peirce (1839-1914) and resultant misunderstandings by his friend and comrade-in-arms William James (1842-1910), the better-known proponent of the theory of pragmatism. But despite its derivation from the Greek *pragma*, practice, and its relationship to modern pragmatism as application- and object-related orientation to what is useful, appropriate and real, the theory of American pragmatism underwent an enormous transformation with the statement that every theory serves a practice and this practice is the measure of the truth of the theory. Peirce, who called pragmatism a scientific method of clarifying concepts, aimed to establish a theory of reality independent of traditional epistemological positions

and to use it to eliminate the sharp distinction between theoretical and practical philosophy once and for all.[3]

The birthplace of pragmatism was the so-called Metaphysical Club in Cambridge, which regularly gathered half a dozen young scholars around Charles S. Peirce and William James in the 1870s.

The provocative concept "metaphysics" was chosen at the time, when philosophical idealism was threatening to collapse, because they believed that it could be transformed into an exact and at the same time democratic science. American pragmatism was the American rebellion against the dogmatic idealism of Europe with its linguistic aestheticism, sublimating everyday things to the point of unrecognizability from the "monastery perspective", a stance that had been perceived as authoritarian and anachronistic since Ralph Waldo Emerson (1813–1882) and the Transcendentalists. Ludwig Marcuse's objection that this American "fresh-air thinking" was intrinsically contradictory, that something like this could not exist, as reflection is driven not by political will but the will for understanding, leads to the conclusion that Americans turned against the dusty abstractions of the philosophical "secret doctrine" because they were more interested in solutions than redemptions.[4] The aim is not differentiation, but applicability. American trust lived in the name of democracy is set against European restlessness.

The first seminal attempt to formulate pragmatism was made by Peirce in his essays "The fixation of belief" (1877) and "How to make our ideas clear" (1878). Indeed his question about clarity introduced a new chapter in the history of the Enlightenment in that he no longer demanded reason for the clarification of concepts, but experiments for the clarification of reason. This conclusion was preceded by Peirce's "Theory of Cognition" (1868), with an early insight into the impossibility of Cartesian doubt. He

Chicago's grid plan after James Thompson, 1834 map with the Kinzie Addition north and the Walcott Addition north-east of the Chicago River.

21

says here that we are not in a position to philosophize on the basis of a rigorous doubt, but need the basis of existing prejudices. These prejudices cannot be removed by a maxim, as they are things that we did not feel we could question. Consequently a priori scepticism must be mere self-deception and not real doubt. Peirce made it clear that scientific scepticism about something definite is mistrustful only for a certain reason. Thinking builds on something that is taken for granted and leads from a discovered contradiction to a justified doubt, which again prepares a new conviction, a new prejudice. For Peirce doubting was not methodological doubting, but living doubting.

With this turn in the philosophical tradition, pragmatism made the mediation of theory and practice into a subject for reflection in the face of the uncertain future in the age of industrialization. It expresses the fact – even though certainty about the temporary nature in principle of every theory did not come until later – that the world is not a complete cosmos, that life has to be lived forwards and that philosophy cannot recognize the nature of things in modest contemplation, as though the laws of nature of the changing world could be determined a priori, in order to orientate the practice to the theory only at that point.

The action involved in Peircian pragmatism is systematic trying out, the original pragmatic determination of the practice of experimental acting for the sake of insight and truth. Peirce suggests that the sense and meaning of a thought lie in the mode of action that it evokes. It is only when the practical effect of an object is weighed up that complete clarity is achieved for the thought.

In pragmatism, in the sense of a "practical effect" concepts relating to a "conditional translation" transform themselves into hypotheses that are scientifically confirmed or disproved by their empirical, experimental conclusions. This way leads to a unity of philosophy and science, of theory and practice, that is able to function. Practice becomes scientific experiment and pragmatism becomes a method of experimental philosophy under which truth is functionalized, can be examined and as a consequence

becomes temporary. Pragmatism's closeness to critical idealism and Peirce's analysis of Kant's Critique of Pure Reason are clearly in evidence here, and again expressed by the naming of his method. Nevertheless Peirce's early formulations contain the roots of later misunderstandings that have contributed to the distortion and vulgarization of pragmatism. When he views the possible meaning of a thought "for the conduct of life" as the exclusive value of that thought he is preparing the way for ranking all action above thought, a development from which he tried to distance himself by finding a new word for his method, pragmaticism.

Whether it is called pragmatism or pragmaticism, both are united in their opposition to transcendental rationalism by the fact that they drive open questions out of the world of thinking by declaring that metaphysicians' unscientific answers are the product of unclear thought. With the maxim that only those questions that can have scientific answers are sensible, the pragmatists simply avoid all those mysterious questions about the course of history that they are just as incapable of solving as their opponents.

But the system that was praised and attacked as pragmatism in America and Europe until well into the 20th century is neither Peirce's massive bundle of thoughts, which did not enjoy lively attention and increasing esteem until the 60s, nor the simplifying theories of William James, but the work of the educationalist John Dewey (1859-1952), who linked pragmatism with materialism and behaviourism, thus creating a kind of American *Weltanschauung*. Dewey was appointed director of the department of philosophy at the newly founded University of Chicago in 1894. This gave him the chance to do some work in the social sphere, and he soon founded an experimental school of psychological and educational studies that became well known far beyond Chicago as the "Dewey School".

Dewey's universally applicable philosophy is based on trust in technical and scientific progress and a positive assessment of instrumental reason. This brought him negative criticism in Germany, particularly from Theodor W. Adorno and Max Horckhei-

Pine Street (now North Michigan Avenue) 1887, view to the north from Huron Street with the Perry H. Smith residence and the Water Tower in the background.

mer, and for a long time fed the European prejudice about the relevance- and action-oriented American society, whose striving for happiness was purely material in nature. Europeans, labouring under the delusions of utopian realism, still look with sceptical admiration at the generous materialism that

puts the Americans in a position to make commerce serve culture and education, and so-called material things like museums, libraries and schools.

Pragmatism in Architecture and Urban Development: Chicago

American tradition did not begin until the Americans freed themselves completely from political dependence on Europe and were able to apply their open way of thinking, feeling, planning, organizing and building to their very particular life conditions and aims without the mediocrity of imitation. A historical approach to the place of the new Museum of Contemporary Art (MCA) in Chicago near north side is like an approach to the American mentality.[5] Even the English liberal Richard Cobdan, a vehement critic of cities, called Chicago the place most worth seeing in the United States, along with Niagara Falls. He said that this great city of 300,000 inhabitants had been created in a mere 40 years on a marshy prairie; at the end of the Civil War (1861-65) it be-

came a railway junction and world-wide trans-shipment centre for cattle, grain and building timber. A second Chicago was created with equal élan after the great fire of 1871, as a "phoenix from the ashes" (Condit), so to speak.

The dense pine forest that once gave its name to the fashionable Chicago shopping street North Michigan Avenue has been pushed back by the city and its imposing sea of skyscrapers. Pine Street was planned in 1834 in the so-called Walcott Addition to James Thompson's plan, who had been asked by the Canal Commissioners in 1830 to create a shape for the future metropolis. As has been customary since Thomas Jefferson's systematization, Thompson based the city's ground plan on a grid, which extended north of the Chicago River for the first time beyond the original settlement around Fort Dearborn, up to Chicago Avenue and the forest boundary, which had moved back. When the city with the beautiful name derived from the Indian Che-ca-gon (wild onions) acquired city rights on 5 August 1833, the actual development was in fact restricted to a total of twelve blocks between the Chicago River from north to south and between State Street and Wells Street from east to west – the later Loop. But by the mid 20th century the world's largest city on a right-angled grid plan with streets over 28 miles long had developed from these beginnings.

The great fire of 1871 broke out in a shingle building in De Koven Street in the south-west of the city and spread very rapidly north and north-east through the city, fanned by a violent south-east wind. But the disaster was also an opportunity for a new start. Pine Street soon became a prestigious residential street for the upper echelons. Magnificent urban villas in historicist styles fringed the tree-lined street, which was carefully paved with wooden blocks.

23

Pine Street began to change after the First World War. Expansion was planned on the basis of the 1909 Burnham Plan, and made a direct connection to the Loop by a bridge that linked Pine Street to Michigan Avenue with an unavoidable kink, making it North Michigan Avenue from then on. Now that it had become a boulevard it was impossible to stop its enhancement and transformation into a commercial district. The boulevard acquired its first striking buildings in the early 20s in the form of the Wrigley Building in the south and the Drake Hotel at the northern end. They gave the district a new architectural identity and prescribed future urban development. The spectacular competition for the Tribune Tower in 1922 and the completion of the neo-Gothic building in 1925 were unmistakable signs of a new era for Chicago. The Second World War meant a brief gap in the development. But as early as 1947 developer Arthur Rubloff commissioned a new development plan from the Holabird & Root architects' office, though it was never realized. It envisaged low street-edge development with a narrow green strip and a second row of buildings behind.

The socio-economic restructuring that started in the 60s in the historic central area, the Loop, led to increased promotion of the alternative commercial centre in the North Michigan Avenue area, where a building boom began that was to last for over twenty years. The unique quality of the Magnificent Mile is due not just to commercial variety but also to the urban development quality that came into being through the impressive concentration of high-rise, big-city architecture over a manageable stretch of only a mile.

In the midst of all the signs of fresh starts and modernity stands the Old Chicago Water Tower, built by W.W. Boyington with the Pumping Station in 1869, on what was then the edge of the city, the junction of Pine Street and Chicago Avenue. Its kitschy, romanticizing neo-Gothic style with rustication is still touchingly reminiscent of the time before the fire; it was one of the few stone buildings to survive. With the assistance of a 138 foot standpipe it had to balance the water pressure in the water pumped east from the Pumping Station opposite, which is now done by the most up-to-date technology in the place.

This symbol of the city's history was treated with due deference. The Old Water Tower is allowed to remain on a plot in a building block fragment between Chicago Avenue and Pearson Street, without reservation and with dignity. Thus in this area of streets an east-west urban axis has formed that starts at the present North Michigan Avenue, points out to the great lake, and is interrupted by only one transverse street, Mies van der Rohe Way, formerly Seneca Street. Burnham's unrealized Plan of Chicago (1909) would have further enhanced the emphasis on this axis by widening Chicago Avenue and continuing it in a magnificent and prestigious pier.

Seneca Park with its little fire station dating from 1902 and the Lake Shore Park, in which there used to be a historical park pavilion close to the shore, change this strange part of the city into a peaceful green zone amidst Chicago's lively office and business quarter; a kind of canyon, as Josef P. Kleihues sees it, which transforms the reflected light as it changes through the day into a play of colours with its framing high-rise façades. This is the place for the new MCA building, which fits in between Mies van der Rohe Way and Fairbanks Court, and giving the Old Water Tower an opposite number that opens up to it generously.

The Place
The museum site is not just new, it is young as well. When excavating for the foundations workers came across remains of the old pier that used to lead out into Lake Michigan beyond the Pumping Station. All

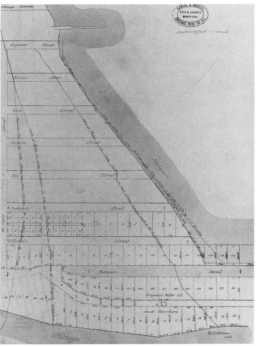

Map of land reclamation in Chicago near north side with the shorelines of 1821, 1833, 1859 and 1877.

the land east of Pine Street, more precisely from St. Clair Street to the present Lake Shore Drive, from the Chicago River in the south to Oak Street in the north is reclaimed land, laboriously wrested from the lake in various stages up to the 1890s. According to a suggestion by surveyor George W. Wilson dating from 1894, the original shoreline in Meander Avenue should have been allowed to remain, but an irrational street pattern of that kind was not compatible with the right-angled grid.

Large areas of the reclaimed land were not built on until well into the 20th century. In 1916-17 the only monumental building, the First Cavalry Armory (then Second Artillery Armory and National Guard Armory) was built on the axis of the Water Tower on the site of the present MCA, to plans by the distinguished Chicago architects' office Holabird & Roche.[6] The building history remains opaque to the present day, but there were numerous interruptions to the work and changes of plan. A start was made with the end building pointing east: an unusual new typological creation, whose body is reminiscent of the nave of a Gothic cathedral with round-arched windows, although the "buttressing" mutated into strange compound piers. The square indoor riding school or arena was not realized by Holabird & Roche, but under state architect Martin, between 1923 and 1926. In the 30s the complex was extended on the western side by architect Milton Eichberg, in a style of insensitive monumentalism of neoclassical provenance. The Armory was pulled down in 1993 to make room for the MCA building.

The Green City

The new MCA building will do justice to its particular urban situation in the city canyon with small, somewhat neglected park and sports facilities not only because it is conceived integratively, but also thanks to its sculpture garden, which subtly links the public role of an art museum with the Chicago tradition of urban parks.

land was acquired before the fire of 1871. This early date raises the urgent question of whether the initiators were familiar with the 1859 Barcelona expansion plan or whether the conceptual relationship in the two plans was merely a timely coincidence that was "in the air" as a result of previous criticism of cities by urban hygienists and social utopians. (And we must not forget that Robert Owen's experimental New Harmony settlement in Indiana, dating from the 1820s, was in view of Chicago in terms of both time and distance.) Ildefonso Cerdà's first and extremely progressive European attempt at ordering an industrial city in urban development terms is based on a greened grid structure and the creation of large parks which, at a distance of 1500 metres, were to have been reached from any point in the town in the shortest possible time. In contrast with Chicago, this project for the public good in Barcelona fell prey to the citizens' private material

Illinois National Guard Armory, first building by Holabird & Roche, view from the East c. 1918-20.

Chicago's park system was the result of hard persuasion in terms of a city that grew so quickly that keeping green spaces open must have seemed almost absurd. Lewis Mumford described the city in the early 1870s as "a brutal network of industrial necessities".[7] Most of the accommodation was in miserable huts, suffocated by railway lines, shunting yards, warehouses, factories, slaughterhouses, grain stores and spoil heaps. But economic requirements made its clear that highly developed architecture was needed, which was possible thanks to the creative spirit and intellectual climate of the city, and produced the Chicago School of Architecture, which pointed the way forward both artistically and in terms of building technology.

The idea of incorporating a system of parks arose as early as the 1860s, when a movement formed to create a ring of parks around the city. The starting point was to be Lincoln Park in the north, and the end the Jackson and Washington South Parks; Humboldt, Central and Douglas Park in the east with green boulevards as links were to complete the ring. The

interests in a sorry fashion, and so only the grid pattern of the street network survived from the original concept.

By including the rail network in the planning Chicago aimed to make the parks accessible to the city's residents within a realistic time-frame. Parks were seen as the most urgent recreational requirement, followed in second place by museums and libraries. The system of parks that thus came into being in Chicago was seen as unique by Europeans, and was still considered exemplary after the turn of the century. The important Berlin architectural critic Werner Hegemann was full of praise when he wrote in the occasion of the 1912 International Urban Development Exhibition in Düsseldorf: "American attempts by educated and socially aware people to learn to assess the horrors of overpopulated urban quarters usefully by taking up permanent residence there provided new openings for understanding the needs of these districts and created the preconditions for success in later organizing these highly innovative playgrounds."[8] In this context Hegemann pointed out the German influence that had come from the kindergartens with their heaps of sand and affected small children in American cities. "In 1893 the first play opportunities on undeveloped building sites were opened by philanthropists in Chicago. In 1898 the city granted 1000 dollars for playgrounds." In 1920 the distinguished art historian A.E. Brinckmann noted that the first hesitant steps had been taken towards imitating Chicago's grandiose system of parks connected by strips of green for play and sport in Germany, in Berlin and Düsseldorf, for example. He wrote: "It is only a linked system of this kind that makes it possible to go for long walks completely surrounded by nature ... These woods extend into the inner city almost like feelers. They automatically provide green wedges that drive nature into the city and that force they way through the entire city centre in thin cracks."[9] Even the particularly critical French urban historian Pierre Lavedan acknowledged the democratic act of the people of Chicago as being the first to have recognized the importance of recreational facilities for the whole population on a sociological basis.[10]

A Recreation Commission was set up alongside the Park Commission, responsible for covering the city with small play- and sports-grounds, "at so-called perambulator distance, in other words at most 10 minutes from every building" (Hegeman). In 1934 134 green areas were equipped with 83 sets of recreation facilities, and over 52 boulevards and parkways formed a linked green band 162 miles long. The idea suggested in 1894 of developing the Michigan Lake Front as a promenade was merely a further step within these public efforts for the common good, under which industry was taken back from the lake despite prime material interests, according to Lavedan. Daniel H. Burnham's concept, conceived in 1897, for "beautifying" Chicago, which led to the 1909 Plan of Chicago, included both an immense park along the lake shore and a gigantic network of tree-lined boulevards.[11]

Everyday Culture

Although a large part of the documents on Chicago's cultural past were irrevocably lost in the 1871 fire, some surviving information show that this was a cosmopolitan, culturally interested and committed society.[12] Even immediately after the city was founded, in the 1830s the city had, as well as a bookshop, a theatre and a newspaper (Chicago Daily American), three debating societies and a regular range of concerts. The Chicago Historical Society was founded in 1856. Fine art was promoted through regular exhibitions from 1859, and artistic

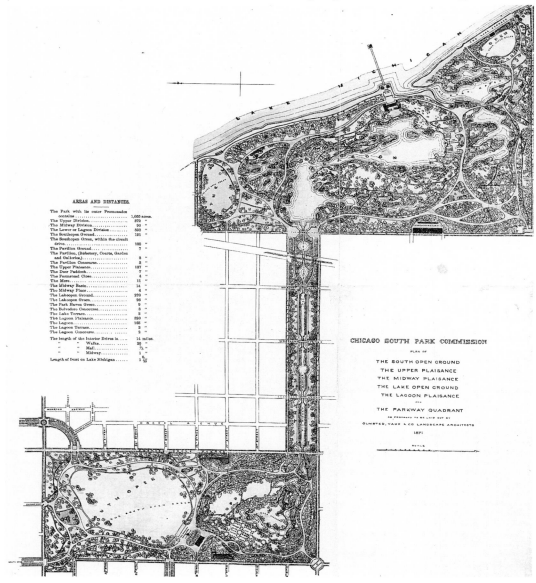

Jackson and Washington Parks in south Chicago with connecting boulevard, 1871.

training was available after the Chicago Academy of Design was founded in 1866. This rapidly expanding school was absorbed into the Art Institute of Chicago with the first art museum and was a high point in the interest shown by Chicago's citizens from the earliest years in producing, collecting and exhibiting art. An example from more recent times is the foundation of the Museum of Contemporary Art in 1967; its first building in East Ontario Street was covered up by Christo for his first building wrap two years later. Even in the 19th century the nucleus of public institutions in Chicago was the result of private actions by well-to-do families who lived in a cultivated fashion and undertook educational trips to Europe. The lively intellectual life made citizens receptive to new ideas and encouraged their enthusiasm in implementing them. In self-critical historical analyses this lively interest in intellectual debate was always seen as a balancing counterweight to the materialistic leitmotif in the city's development.

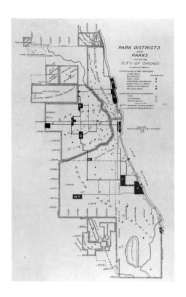

System of parks within the city of Chicago in 1913.

1   Cf. Lewis Mumford, Roots of Contemporary American Architecture. A series of thirty-seven essays dating from the mid-nineteenth century to the present, New York 1972 [1952], in it L. Mumford, A Backward Glance.
2   About Bertrand Russell see Ludwig Marcuse, Amerikanisches Philosophieren. Pragmatisten, Polytheisten, Tragiker (1959), Zurich 1994, p. 121.
3   Charles S. Peirce, Über die Klarheit unserer Gedanken/How to Make Our Ideas Clear. Edited by Klaus Oehler, Frankfurt/M. 1968.
4   Ludwig Marcuse, loc. cit., p. 17 ff.

5   Cf. Paul Gilbert and Charles Lee Bryson, Chicago and its makers, Chicago 1929; Harold M. Mayer and Richard C. Wade, Chicago: Growth of a Metropolis, Chicago/London 1969.
6   Cf. The American Architect, vol. CXVIII, no. 2339, Oct. 20, 1920; Robert Bruegmann, Holabird & Roche. Holabird & Root. An Illustrated Catalog of Works, vol. II, 1911-1927, New York/London 1991, p. 98 ff.
7   Quoted from Carl W. Condit, The Chicago School of Architecture. A History of Commercial and Public Building in the Chicago Area 1875-1925, Chicago/London 1964, p. 16.
8   Werner Hegemann (ed.), Der Städtebau

nach den Ergebnissen der Allgemeinen Städtebau-Ausstellung in Berlin nebst einem Anhang: Die Internationale Städtebau-Ausstellung in Düsseldorf, Berlin 1913, p. 354.
9   A.E. Brinckmann, Stadtbaukunst. Geschichtliche Querschnitte und neuzeitliche Ziele, Berlin-Neubabelsberg 1920, p. 132.
10   Cf. Pierre Lavedan, Histoire de l'Urbanisme. Époque Contemporaine, Paris 1952.
11   Cf. Daniel H. Burnham and Edward H. Bennett, Plan of Chicago, Chicago 1909.
12   Cf. Carl W. Condit, loc. cit., chapter II.

Burnham & Root
(north 1891)/Holabird
& Roche (south 1893),
Monadnock Building.

Notes on the Chicago
School of Architecture

German response to the so-called Chicago School of Architecture began in the 1890s with individual publications on skyscrapers in the USA, but they presented the new type mainly as a spectacle. The eclecticism of the designs was singled out for particular criticism, but their technical mastery was completely acknowledged. After 1893, i.e. in connection with the Chicago World Fair, major treatises appeared in German building magazines, and Paul Graef produced a detailed documentation of American building culture for the turn of the century, but did not include skyscrapers. Skyscrapers were criticized into the twenties because of what Europeans perceived as deficiencies in terms of urban development and function, but above all because of their lack of aesthetic independence. One exception was Henry Hobson Richardson's romanticism, which was allowed to have a certain independence.

And so the new development in America was noticed in Germany at a very early stage, but there was no concentrated analysis until it was also possible to build skyscrapers in Europe. A series of articles about the "World in a Hundred Years" in the "Deutsche Illustrierte Zeitung" in 1908 had a clear influence. They were illustrated with drawings by Ernst Lübbert associating skyscrapers with fantasies of progress in transport technology. However, the practical way to the skyscraper in Germany took the detour of industrial building and was given crucial impetus by Walter Gropius's interest in American grain stores, which began roughly at the time of the publication of the influential work on Frank Lloyd Wright in 1910[1] and led to his subsequent professorship in Harvard via his entry for the "Chicago Tribune" Tower in 1922.

Admiration was drawn from architects in the Deutscher Werkbund and those who were later close to the Bauhaus by the functionalism derived from the idea of a building articulated mainly by its construction, which is true of some of the "Chicago School" buildings. As far as office buildings were concerned, they were dealing with something that was a relatively young genre at the time, which had not developed until the service industry started to grow in the 19th century. In this sense the office skyscraper appeared as a symbol of the new world in Germany even in the twenties and in view of the European crises in the years between the wars as the sign of an industrial nation striving for progress. Mass culture was also perceived as an element of new democratic achievements, particularly by the political left, while conservatives warned against Americanization of the intellect. Progressive forces committed to Modernism saw leitmotifs of their endeavours for renewal in the "new ideas" conveyed by American city culture.

Jenney's First Leiter Building

The First Leiter Building is particularly significant among the early "Chicago School" buildings. It was designed by William LeBaron Jenney in 1879, eight

years after the disastrous fire that destroyed large parts of the city, and is generally considered to be the first "Chicago School" building. The building is notable for its lucid structure, which makes the building's grid visible on its façade. Jenney refrained almost completely from articulating a façade, and essentially restricted himself to reproducing the vertical and horizontal bands determined by the support structure. He also went against the convention of the times by using almost no ornamental decoration. Until then this had been possible only for industrial buildings, and even there it was an exception. It was precisely this lack of decoration that always suggested the understanding that this build-

ing of Jenney's expressed understanding of an aesthetic programme on which it was based. But this assessment seems questionable if one bears in mind that Jenney was trained in France as a structural engineer and for design questions had to rely on colleagues in his office, which had existed since 1871.[2] The building was above all the product of a style that had not yet been developed and attracted attention largely because it anticipated the stripping of buildings on the basis of orientation towards industrial building practices. The design was driven not by a new will for design, but by the economic constraints expressed in a certain lack of aesthetic

intention that was to pervade Jenney's future designs as well. If his Home Insurance Building of 1884, the 1890 Fair Store or the Manhattan Building he designed in 1890 are taken for comparison, it becomes clear that he did not perceive simplicity of aesthetic expression as a quality in its own right. Instead Jenney, along with many of his contemporaries, made an inadequate attempt of creating a satisfactory expression for the new technical and typological requirements by going back to historic models. These are, as well as Renaissance palazzi, preferred above all by Henry Robson Richardson because of their character as block development as a peripheral conclusion, the historical formal vocabulary of the beaux arts aesthetic, which was used in the Home Insurance Building and, in even more questionable form, in the Fair Store.[3]

Despite his unsatisfactory aesthetic experiments Jenney does deserve credit for having considerably influenced the structural development of the Chicago School with these buildings. The First Leiter Building is still a comparatively conventional construction. Here the ceilings are supported by iron bearers on which the wooden beams of the ceilings are laid, while the supporting frames between the windows stand on stone parapets formed by the brick piers. The construction has hardly any extension-resistant connections, so that it is not possible to talk about a genuine frame. The lack of congruence between technical innovation and external appearance that characterizes the whole development of the "Chicago School" appears all the more strongly here. Technically progressive buildings are hidden behind stone cladding, while traditional buildings seem to reflect new concepts. The basis

l.: Henry Hobson Richardson, Marshall Field Wholesale Store, 1885-87, the rusticated masonry and the tectonics of the building are reminiscent of Renaissance palazzi.

r.: Giuliano da Sangallo, Palazzo Strozzi, Florence 1489/90.

Ernst Lübbert, Die Stadt der Zukunft (The City of the Future), 1908; early European visions of large cities are based on motifs from American cities.

for the development of the constructive system that finally gave the Home Insurance Building its breakthrough was laid by various inventions in the USA, by James Bogardus and Daniel Badger in New York, for example, and above all by French engineers like Gustave Eiffel. The Home Insurance Building is completely supported by an iron skeleton and to a

certain extent allots only a protective function to the façade, which is now freed of its support function. Jenney's 1890 Manhattan Building, with Burnham & Root's Rand McNally Building, is the first universal skeleton construction, with a façade also supported by a steel frame.

In this way the First Leiter Building remained an exception for years in terms of the functionality of its design. Even if there were a few buildings in the next ten years whose appearance depended on their support structure and the potential of that structure was used entirely within the spirit of the building needed, it is reasonable only to a limited extent to talk of the pragmatism of the functionalism that is so often invoked.

To avoid showing that criticism of the eclecticism of American skyscrapers that was so frequently expressed in Europe well into the nineteen-twenties at this point, attention should be drawn to buildings by Burnham & Root, for example, that were built around 1890, before the death of John Wellborn Root,[4] including the north section of the Monadnock Building,[5] and those buildings by Holabird & Roche that indicate at the turn of the century that lasting emancipation from the claims of prestige and thus permanent renunciation of ornament are winning through. This partnership's architecture is programmatically restricted at this time to articulation by structural elements and thus shows itself to be capable of connection with further development in Europe. The time gap between the theoretical articulation of functionalism by Horatio Greenough (1805-1852) and its taking effect architecturally ends with buildings like the Marquette Building 1893-1894, the McClurg Building 1899-1900, 325 West

Jackson Boulevard 1904-1911, the Republic Building 1905-1906 (formerly at 209 South State Street; demolished in 1961) or the Brooks Building 1909-1910 and similar projects.

Sullivan and Functionalism

Sullivan's credo "form follows function" has with its history of many misinterpretations also led to an idealized assessment of the "Chicago School". As far as forming the theory of an architecture interested in objective functionality is concerned, the writings of Greenough and later, among Sullivan's contemporaries, those of his partners Dankmar Adler and John Wellborn Root are considerably more important. The suggestive power of the motto has in many places concealed the fact that Sullivan's function concept cannot be made to agree with the demand of giving up ornament, and that the apparent contradiction with his own designs is in fact unsubstantiated.

Overall this has meant that the direct aesthetic consequences of the so-called "Chicago School" have been overestimated. Ultimately it is clear in the majority of the designs that this architecture can really be considered as the conclusion of a story of attempts that failed aesthetically to make new building problems harmonize with adequate representation forms.

Despite this, the "Chicago School" had a large number of consequences, as viewed from the 20th century its interpretation became effective as a bridge to the avant-garde despite substantial load-bearing capacity and complemented various developments in European countries with the aspect of a programmatic demand for direct expression of the construction. The 19th century was not yet in a position to ignore the claims of prestige architecture. This was left to New Building in the twenties in Europe and architects like Walter Gropius, Mies van der Rohe, Ludwig Hilberseimer, Alvar Aalto and J.J.P. Oud, who achieved formal reduction down to the structural elements.

William LeBaron Jenney, First Leiter Building, 1879.

William LeBaron Jenney, Home Insurance Building, 1885-85.

Theoretical Analysis of 19th Century Architecture in the USA

An obvious point of reference to the discussion about the American contribution to functionalism is offered by the theoretical reflections made forty years before the work of the Chicago School of Architecture began. It is mainly a matter of the functional-organic nature philosophy of Ralph Waldo Emerson (1803-82), which was further developed by American sculptor Horatio Greenough (1805-52) in particular, who lived mainly in Italy. Greenough, who met Emerson in Florence in 1833, and whose own thinking worked back into the late Emerson's way of looking at things, formulated his position with the intention of developing a genuinely American architectural style. His closeness to Emerson seems clear particularly when he saw the basis of this style in a direct recourse to the laws of nature. He was guided here by an understanding of skin and skeleton that was influenced by anatomy, which as is well known became one of the basic ideas of functionalist architecture in the form of skeleton and cladding. Greenough thought about the notion of function himself in the treatise "Relative and Independant Beauty", which he wrote after 1850. There he developed the idea of a specifically American architecture based on a scientifically shaped concept of function that has been made absolute, which causes nature to appear as a sum of functions. In terms of architecture the concept was stretched so far that aesthetic and moral aspects could be made part of it as well. Just as recourse to nature's scientifically recorded conformity to law was intended to be a guarantee of emancipation from the hierarchic social order of absolutism for the philosophy of the Enlightenment, nature was now claimed by Ameri-

Burnham & Root (north 1891)/Holabird & Roche (south 1893), Monadnock Building; the detail shows clearly the increasingly thick masonry in the base area of the building (right), which is not needed in the technically more modern construction (left).

can theoreticians as a reference point for liberation from the cultural legacy of the Old World, which was seen as a fetter.

The essential functionality of a building reduced to its basic components, i.e. also a complete renunciation of decoration, became a positive value that guaranteed aesthetic quality, if only function was optimized within it. One feels oneself reminded of the economy precept of the French architectural theoretician Jean-Nicolas-Louis Legrand (1760-1834), which was interpreted by Greenough in a moral sense and in this way could be claimed as an American national virtue.

The question of a specifically American architecture acquired new relevance as architecture students turned to Europe, above all to the École des Beaux–Arts. After Richard Morris Hunt became the first American to enrol at the school in Paris in 1846, a period of study in the French capital became an obligatory component of an ambitious American architect's training. Hunt was followed by Henry Hobson Richardson (1838-86) among others, and also Sullivan, as is well known; he studied in Paris in the seventies. Overall interplay between America and Europe was reinforced in the second half of the century, so that American architectural theory increasingly came under the influence of the École des Beaux–Arts, while autonomous American architecture developed above all in the country and the suburbs.

New expectations of art and architecture, which were very important for the Americans' search for their own national style, formulated since the beginning of the century, were conveyed especially in lectures by Hippolyte Taine, who was Professor of Building History at the École. Taine suggested that specific artistic solutions that documented the condition of the particular culture were to be found for every period. Every artistic problem should find its own individual expression and be represented dressed in its own forms. Instead of the validity of a style regardless of time on the basis of academic rules, here steps were already being taken on the

Holabird & Roche, Cable Building 1898-99; it is not until this period that buildings again reach the reduction of building ornament shown by Jenney's First Leiter Building, although against a different background.

path that understands the results of architectural creativity as an objective solution to a given problem. This presents an important point of contact with the aesthetics of the "Chicago School". Finally Sullivan had also linked his famous credo with his training at this school. In a letter to Claude Bragdon dated 25 July 1904 he wrote: "It was certainly in the school [École des Beaux–Arts], and because of the teachings of the school, that there entered my mind, fructified in my mind, the germ of thet law which later, after much observation of nature´s processes, I formulated in the phrase, 'Form follows Function' ".

Louis H. Sullivan,
Carson Pirie Scott
Store, 1899.

1   *Frank Lloyd Wright, Ausgeführte Bauten und Entwürfe, Berlin 1910.*
2   *William Holabird and Martin Roche worked in Jenney's office from 1875 to 1879.*
3   *The architectural magazine "Inland Architect and News Record" is generally seen as the organ of the "Chicago School". Looking through the relevant volumes gives a picture that by no means suggests the conclusion that the architects subsumed under this concept had the self-confidence of an avant-garde. The majority of the projects presented were tradi-*
tional masonry structures a very few storeys high: residential buildings, stations, churches and the like. The now famous skyscraper buildings of that time are as rare as contributions showing an interest in construction by Dankmar Adler or more or less programmatic contributions by Louis H. Sullivan or John Wellborn Roots, who were both on the editorial board for a few years.
4   *It became clear that this influence was due to Root in particular, who also made fundamental theoretical contributions to the*
"Chicago School", when Burnham effortlessly moved back to the historicizing aesthetic of the early period after the death of his partner.
5   *The building consists of two parts built a few years apart. The aesthetic functionalism of the older north section is generally seen as proof that traditional masonry (in this case 6 feet thick on the ground floor) is unsuitable for high buildings, while the later south section, designed by Holabird & Roche, is influenced by the familiar eclecticism, although technically it is a modern skeleton construction.*

33

Mies van der Rohe,
Lake Shore Drive Apart-
ments, view while
under construction.

German Architects in Chicago

The fact that Mies van der Rohe moved from Berlin to Chicago of all places in 1938 may, as Franz Schulze suggests,[1] have been partly because Gropius, after unsuccessful negotiations between the Dean of the College of Architecture at Harvard University, Joseph Hudnut, and Mies in 1936, was preferred for appointment to a chair of architecture. On the other hand it is no coincidence that Chicago was on the agenda as a place to which he might emigrate. Apart from the many tasks that awaited him there, Mies van der Rohe was simply the best-known of a series of German architects who had worked in Chicago since the mid 19th century.

During a stay in Jackson Hole, Wyoming, in response to an invitation from Stanley Resor, for whom Mies was designing a house at the time, a conversation took place between John A. Holabird and Mies. Holabird was the son of the founder of one of the most important architects' offices in Chicago, Holabird & Roche, and himself a distinguished architect, had been commissioned by the Armour (later Illinois) Institute of Technology to negotiate with Mies about directing the architecture department there. Mies accepted at once and arrived in Chicago in 1938. However logical this step may possibly seem, as there was a widely-held view – on the basis of Sigfried Giedion's response in his book "Space, Time and Architecture" – that there was a historic connection between the architecture of the Chicago School of Architecture and that of the New Building movement in Germany, Mies himself always disputed this connection in the statements he made.[2] He did agree in an interview in 1956[3] that he had seen a drawing by Louis H. Sullivan that has interested him at an exhibition in The Hague in 1912, but clearly distanced himself from Sullivan's view of architecture on another occasion.[4] It is not surprising that Mies felt that the idea of a reconciliation between construction and decoration, which was constitutive for Sullivan's self-perception, was no longer up-to-date. To a certain extent the attitude anticipated the changed insight of recent years into the romantic roots of Sullivan's thinking. As well as this, as a Modern architect Mies was simply too little interested in the formation of historical continuity to have been able to identify a strikingly different aesthetic of structural relationships under this surface.

Chicago had about 20,000 inhabitants around 1848. The city's increasing significance as a centre of trade and industry at the northern end of the Illinois-Michigan canal was growing steadily and after 1860 it was additionally enhanced as an important railway junction. The immense need for housing development, but above all for commercial development, drew increasing numbers of members of the building trade to Chicago from the middle of the century. The first architects came from the east coast, like John M. Van Osdel, who is considered the first architect of Chicago; he came from Baltimore in 1837. Meanwhile the workforce consisted increasingly of immigrants from Europe, where the Irish famine of

1846 and also the failed revolution of 1848 in Germany triggered a wave of emigration that continued into the early 20th century. These groups contributed to the rapid growth of the city and made a major contribution to shaping its appearance in the second half of the 19th century.

Let us select just a few of the many architects who worked in Chicago since that time. Frederick Baumann (1826-1921) was one of the first Germans to come to Chicago, in 1850, and was first employed in Van Osdel's office, where Daniel Burnham also worked, as an engineer, and was incidentally much admired by Sullivan.[5] Baumann was born in Angermünd, and had studied in various Prussian trade schools and the Königliches Gewerbeinstitut in Berlin.[6] From 1852-54 he was the partner of Edward Bur-

ling, and after that worked for Osdel again until 1856. Later he directed a building company, made a considerable contribution to architectural development with a book on foundations published in 1873,[7] and entered into a partnership with his cousin Edward Baumann in 1868, which lasted until 1879. In the eighties he published an essay on skyscraper constructions, which Condit thought had influenced Jenney.[8] Baumann's cousin Edward had attended the trade school in Graudenz until 1856 and went to Chicago in the same year. He first worked for Burling and Baumann there, and then, while in partnership with his cousin, was actively involved in rebuilding the city as an architect with overall control. Edward Burling became Dankmar Adler's partner in 1871; Adler was born in Saxony in Germany, came to Chicago in 1861, worked there from 1863 with his fellow-countryman August Bauer (who came from Berlin in 1853) and later became Louis H. Sullivan's partner.

German architect Otto Matz was also more significant for technical than for aesthetic development. He was in Chicago from the 50s, and built the Great Central Station in 1856. His Nixon Building was almost complete when the fire broke out in October 1871. As Matz had clad the iron supports of his

building with plaster and concrete, which was less than usual at the time in Chicago, the support structuhre survived the fire almost undamaged. The building was cleaned, rubble removed, and it was able to open in the same year. This experience was drawn upon and further developed in subsequent years, when fire safety was understandably a focus of attention. Architects like Alfred S. Altschuler, Adolph Cudell, Fritz Foltz, Arthur Hercz, Edmund C. Krause, Richard E. Schmidt, Hermann Valentin Von Holst, August C. Wilmanns, Arthur Woltersdorf and many others stand for a group of architects, engineers and workmen who settled in Chicago in such numbers, particularly after the "Great Fire", that the city became the greatest colony of German settlers in the American mid-west.

If one considers the influence of German architects and above all engineers on building in Chicago and then the direct effect of Chicago architecture on the skyscraper debate in Germany in the twenties,[9] the relationship between the two places can be seen as a long-lasting and constantly revived interaction that led to a large number of fertile connection, reaching a provisional climax in the lively German involvement in the competition for the "Chicago Tribune" Tower in 1921. Emigration from Nazi Ger-

Mies van der Rohe, Esters House, Krefeld, Germany 1928, façade.

Mies van der Rohe, reinforced concrete office building, design 1922.

Walter Gropius, competition entry for the "Chicago Tribune" Tower, 1922. Gropius combines the principles of Neues Bauen (New Building) in Europe with skyscraper typology and relates to the history of the "Chicago School" with details like the typical windows.

many in the thirties again took a series of German architects and artists, or architects and artists who were working in Germany, to Chicago, including Mies van der Rohe, Ludwig Hilberseimer and Laszlo

Schipporeit & Heinrich, Lake Point Tower, 1968. The building shows some connection with Mies van der Rohe's glass skyscraper design of 1920.

Moholy-Nagy. As Professor of Architecture at the Illinois Institute of Technology (IIT), but also as a busy architect, Mies had a great deal of influence on Chicago architecture and architecture in the United States generally. Direct influence on John Heinrich and George Schipporeit, for example, cannot be overlooked. Both were students at the IIT and later worked in Mies's office. Mies's 1921 design for a skyscraper for Friedrichstraße in Berlin is clearly a source of inspiration for their design for the spectacular Lake Point Tower, built in 1968. Other members of Mies's office like Joseph Fujikawa, Arthur Salzmann, Gene Summers and Mies's grandson Dirk Lohan are internationally known. But the general influence on Chicago design, especially in the sixties and seventies, is obvious. The clearest evidence of analysis of the famous architect's aesthetic is to be found in early designs by the office of Skidmore, Owens and Merryl. The fact that conversely Mies shows evidence that he had come to terms with American architectural practice in his work is clear not only in the fact that he took the opportunity of

Mies van der Rohe, Lake Shore Drive Apartments, 1948-50, general plan. A comparison with the ground plan (see p. 38) shows that the façade articulation shows 4 axes for each section, while the floor tiles show 6 axes. The inserted shear walls relate to neither system, but respond to the desire for optimum use of space.

Mies van der Rohe, glass skyscraper, model 1920/21.

developing the skyscraper type in his very first buildings for Chicago: he also assimilated specific features of American building culture. As well as this, generalization of the function concept from building function to the function of the architectural element in the spirit of rationalist architecture took place in the American period of activity, which was an inevitable consequence of his development path. In Europe Mies was concerned above all with spatial development and the qualities of various materials, in the United States construction rapidly became a vital force in his concept of architecture. The European Mies' asymmetrical designs, apart from the early detached houses before the First World War, are characterized by rejection of traditional sculptural principles. If one takes the Barcelona Pavilion or the reinforced concrete country house as examples, these can be seen to be influenced by the open ground plans of Wright's prairie houses, in other words decidedly American spatial concepts – as well as Expressionism, De Stijl and the possibilities of new technical achievements. The clearly anti-tradi-

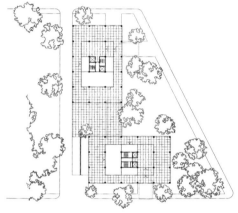

tional claim of his work is first in evidence in buildings that not by chance relate to a building tradition that had developed above all in the United States up to then. These are the designs for glass skyscrapers in Friedrichstadt in Berlin dating from 1919 and 1920/21. Here Mies detached himself from the remnants of traditional building practice for the first time and presented himself as a decidedly modern architect. In 1922 came the design for the reinforced concrete office building, in 1923 the brick country house and in 1924 the reinforced concrete country house. All these works remained projects, but together they demonstrate the imagination with which Mies approached the new materials. The "Afrikanische Straße" estate in Berlin (1926/27) and the residential building in the Weißenhof Estate in Stuttgart (1927) are the projects dating from the twenties, years bedevilled with financial problems, that best show the uncompromising quality of the earlier designs. They gave Mies his first opportunity to implement certain qualities of his designs that he then perfected in the late twenties in his Barcelona Pavilion and the Tugendhat house.

In the early days after his move Mies retained an open concept for his buildings. Examples of this are the general plan for the IIT (1938), the asymmetrical

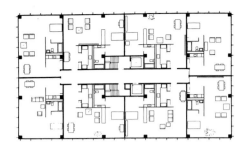

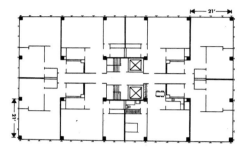

concept for Farnsworth House (1945) and the first ground plan designs for the Lake Shore Drive Apartments, which try out a free ground plan for multi-storey housing. Mies altered this first design for the apartment ground plans on the suggestion of his client, Herbert Greenwald. Greenwald was supposedly impressed by the ground plans, but was afraid that they would not be a commercial success, so that in his second design Mies worked out the good but traditional ground plans that were finally built. This can be put down to the influence of American pragmatism, but anyway it is a case of an attitude freed from idealistic unwillingness to compromise.

With a view to the ideals of architectural rationality conveyed through European culture it is also interesting here that the floor grid, drawn throughout the general plans and demonstrated by the floor tiles in the building neither agrees with the walls in the living areas, which are determined by the need for optimum exploitation, nor with the articulation of the façade. This is determined by sections that each bring four windows together, but do not correspond with the underlying grid. His later American work, the Seagram Building in New York, for example, in contrast with the examples described here, is determined to a certain extent by a return to classical structures in the European style. The building is set back from the Park Avenue building line, thus forming a small square in front, with symmetrically placed pools to guide visitors to the raised central entrance. In order to enter this square, visitors have to climb a short flight of steps to the top of the base on which the skyscraper stands. The building is raised out of the city space by these subtle means, and ennobled with a gesture that is classical to an extent. The influence of the young American architect Philip Johnson, with whom Mies worked on this building, may have been not inconsiderable in terms of updating the European building tradition, but for Mies the desire for what is absent in each case as a motif is clear. While in the twenties Mies criticized traditional European architecture by using American paradigms, he acted conversely in fifties America – but always as part of a dialogue between the two cultures.

Mies van der Rohe, Lake Shore Drive Apartments, first design for the ground floor plan.

Ludwig Mies van der Rohe, Farnsworth House.

1   Franz Schulze, "How Chicago got Mies – and Harvard didn't", Inland Architect 21 (May 1977).

2   Sigfried Giedion in particular suggest the connection between Mies and the "Chicago School"; for this cf. Giedion, Space, Time and Architecture, Cambridge/Mass. 1941. The arguments put forward here are particularly interesting because Giedion, as a German-speaking European, always questions the development in terms of the interaction between Europe and America.

3   Katherine Kuhn, "Mies van der Rohe. Modern Classicist", Saturday Review 48, p. 61.

4   Peter Carter, "Mies van der Rohe. An Appreciation on the Occasion, this month, of his 75th Birthday", Architectural Design 31 (March 1961), p. 4.

5   Cf. Carl W. Condit, The Chicago School of Architecture. A History of Commercial and Public Building in the Chicago Area 1875-1925, Chicago/London 1964, p. 36.

6   Cf. the autobiographical article "Life, Reminiscences and Notes of Frederick Bau-

mann", Construction News 41 (January 15, 1916), pp. 5-6.

7   Frederick Baumann, A Theory of Isolated Pier Foundations, Chicago 1873.

8   Cf. Condit, loc. cit., p. 83.

9   Cf. Dietrich Neumann, Die Wolkenkratzer kommen, Stuttgart 1995.

Documentation

The Museum of Contemporary Art is sited near the historic Water Tower on Mies van der Rohe Way. A green axis has survived since the 19th century in an urban canyon there between Michigan Avenue and Lake Michigan. The building with its sculpture garden is built on a ground plan of two squares fitted together. The entrance façade faces away from the harsh lake shore and opens to the city on the western side.

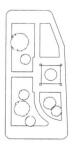
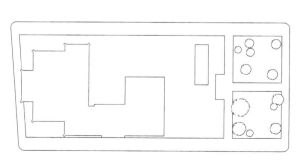
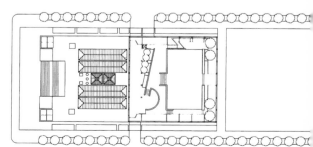

The new museum
building sits between
the skyscrapers in
Chicago Avenue and
Pearson Street as if
an urban canyon.
View east from the
Water Tower over the
Pumping Station to
Lake Michigan.

J.P. Kleihues,
general plan including
the bridge over Lake
Shore Drive, which
was not built.

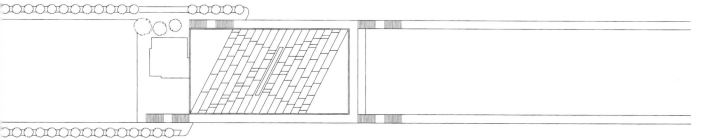

Geometry and modular order

Josef P. Kleihues's designs have a basic structure in common, and all dimensions are derived from these wherever possible. A modular spatial grid determines how to place details, so that there are no arbitrary relations between the parts of the building. In this way the individual parameters of the design work arise from the objective conditions of the place – in Chicago the block structure of the city ground plan, which Kleihues felt obliged to follow – and a striving for ideal proportions in the geometry of a building perceived as autonomous. Kleihues made use of the long dimensions of the plot, almost a double square, for the museum design, by developing the ground plan of the building over two squares, with a axis of 182 by 182 feet.

The MCA building grid is based on a basic module of 2 feet, which add up to units of an axis dimension of 26 feet. For the width of the building seven of these units add up to 182 feet plus a foot on each side to complete the grid element, which is always extreme and constructively conditioned. The same principle is used to develop the height of the building, using two units plus base. The grid inherent in the building is illustrated on the façade by continuous, 2-foot wide bands intersecting at right angles. A square field with an axis dimension of 26 feet, always placed in the middle of the band, reflects the building's constructional grid, while the quartered field with the halved axis dimension corresponds with the horizontal division of the storeys. In the original conception the museum building followed the street-edge development of the plot in the Chicago Avenue, Mies van der Rohe Way and Pearson street with an axis dimension of 196 x 196 feet. But for financial reasons Kleihues was compelled to reduce the amount of built space. However, this step was not to be to the disadvantage of individual functioning areas. Instead of changing the accepted basic structure of the building, he decided on the unusual procedure of reducing the

Ceiling lighting with translucent glass cladding.

The air outlet for the air-conditioning in the offices is slightly raised to prevent office chairs being moved too close to the glass pane.

The American oak door frame fits precisely into the geometrical system of the construction grid.

size of the building. He retained the basic 2-foot module but brought the axial dimension down from 28 to 26 feet, producing a realized length of 184 feet for the edge of the building. When this procedure was examined, a surprising number of advantages were found. It meant that the building was more openly placed, and so a generous square could be realized in front of the building and there could be planting on both sides. And not least, the exhibition areas benefited from the contraction, as the galleries for temporary exhibitions could be realized without supports.

If the base structure is compared with the wall articulation in the contracted version, it can be seen that the ideal-typical geometry has shifted as a result of the process. The square infill elements for the grid in the wall zone deviate from the ideal dimensions of the building. If the axial dimension, reduced to 26 feet, is divided by 2, this gives 13 feet which – again separated by a band 2 feet wide – permit infill elements of 11 feet. These fields are divided into four square slabs, so that each slab has an edge 5 feet 6 inches long. But the articulation of the base is derived from an even structure of square elements the size of the basic module, in other words 2 feet. Thus a shift in the grid structure is produced in relation to the edge zone fields of 5 feet 6 inches, expressed in the fact that the joints alternate in every second field.

This conflict presents a fundamental problem for the European architectural tradition of rationalism, the roots of which can be traced back to the corner conflict in the Doric column order in ancient temples. It results from the European architectural ideal and the striving for beauty and harmony that can be comprehended even in industrial architecture, while in the American tradition of architecture and urban development pragmatically directed decision-making parameters, both economically and functionally, are more in evidence, and always leave room for imposing gestures.

Ground plans

It is especially clear that Kleihues has come to terms with the pragmatism of American design practice, a particularly striking feature of the works of the Chicago School of Architecture, if we consider the overlapping of the various ground plans in the different floors. For complex designs like the Neukölln hospital in Berlin (1973-86) with diverse functional demands he still reacted by excorporating certain functional areas for the sake of harmonizing the ground plans, but he abandoned this principle for the MCA. Accordingly the ground floor and the basement with transversely placed lecture

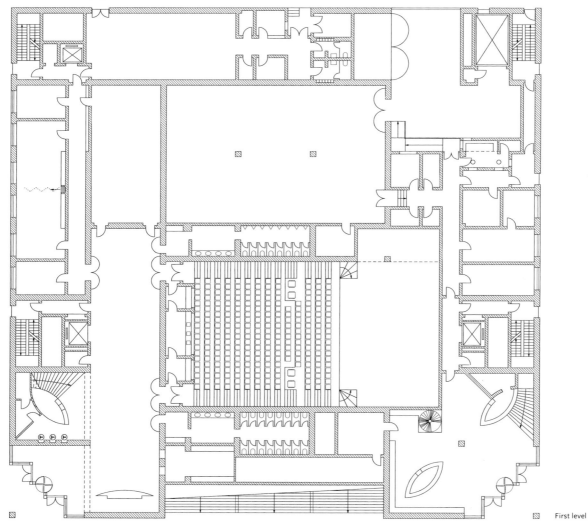

First level

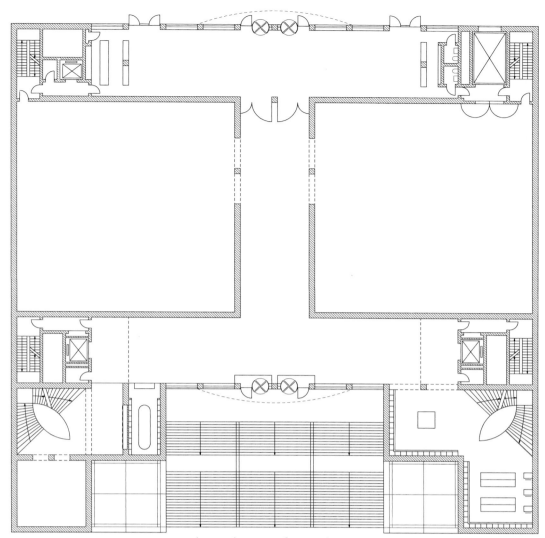

Second level

theatre do not conform to the organizational principles of the rest of the building. This solution arose because it was necessary to make the lecture theatre's opening times independent of those of the rest of the museum and to limit access to the side entrance for the disabled in the north-western part of the building. The basement floor is largely used as a technical control room, but there are some store-rooms and other side-rooms. The rest of the space was used to bring the rows of seats in the lecture theatre down to this level and install a large stage area about 30 feet deep and 52 feet wide.

The ground floor is characterized by its heterogeneous use programme. It contains the side entrances to the museum, which give access to the lecture theatre and to the Robert B. and Beatrice C. Mayer Education Center from Pearson Street. The inner main staircase, which connects all the public areas with each other and is developed to a shipshape form, starts, here, along with the lift.

Analogously with this, on the right-hand, Chicago Avenue side of the building another shipshape staircase provides access to the two-storey bookshop, which is thus connected to the main lobby. A delivery road makes it possible to drive straight through the building and transport delivered works of art to the depot or into the upper storeys, via direct access by the goods lift. The restaurant kitchen, cold-store and storage rooms are on the ground floor, and so is the museum carpark.

The remaining ground plans are determined largely by the ideal-typical symmetrical principle. The museum's exhibition galleries are reached by the external main staircase at second floor level, where the transversely placed main lobby, two storeys high and, adjacent to it, at atrium-like central area, are also to be found; it rises through all floors to the roof of the building and is lit by square skylights.

On both sides of the atrium are the support-free galleries for temporary exhibitions, each of which has a ground area of 76 by 76 feet, and are thus almost 6000 square feet in size. Straight ahead the hall provides a direct connection to the restaurant area, which is also transversely placed, and to the sculpture garden.

In the corner areas facing Mies van der Rohe Way, instead of the third floor there are inserted levels available for offices in the south-west corner and for exhibition areas in the north-east corner.

On the fourth floor, which because of the double floor height in the core area is actually the second museum level, are the galleries for the permanent collection, for video installations and small temporary exhibitions. The two-floor high main galleries, with skylights, for the permanent collection are on both sides of the building axis, laid out as two long, parallel spaces in each case, whose double axis makes it possible to make a circular tour of the exhibition. In the course of this the open connecting corridors between the left and right halves of the gallery open up a view of the

View of the gallery above the main lobby.

View of the gallery opposite.

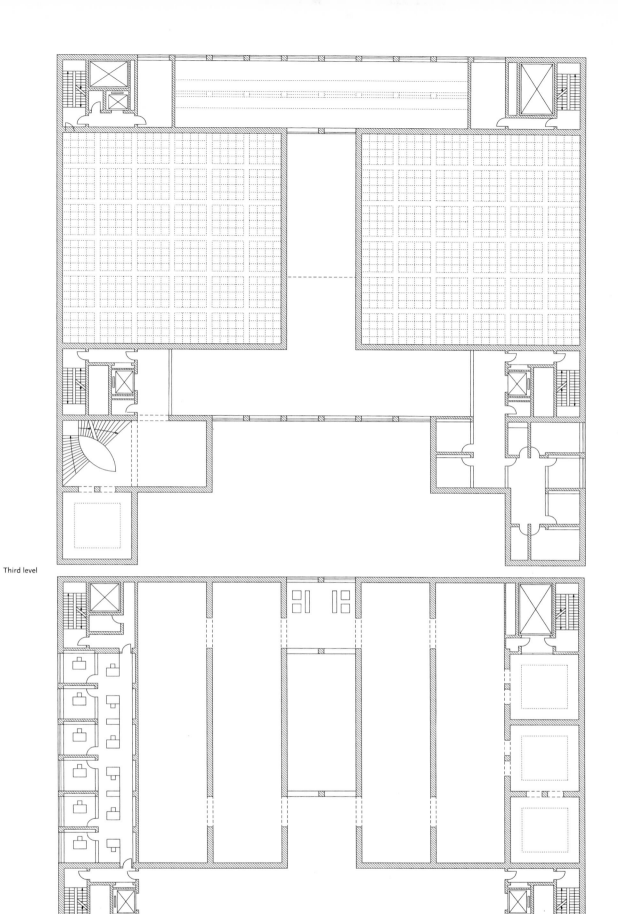

Third level

Fourth level

atrium right down to the entrance level, making it possible to experience the spatial interpenetration of the levels from there as well.

On the façade side of the museum an one-storey gallery above the main lobby provides access to the two smaller exhibition spaces, which are each in corner areas and are specially suitable for special installations or for presenting works on paper.

A so-called mezzanine floor has been installed above this level as well. It has a U-shaped ground plan and includes the four glass-vaulted exhibition halls for the permanent collection and the central hall, which rises through three full floors. On this mezzanine, or fifth, floor are offices, the directorial offices and a large conference room.

Roofscape with view of Lake Michigan.

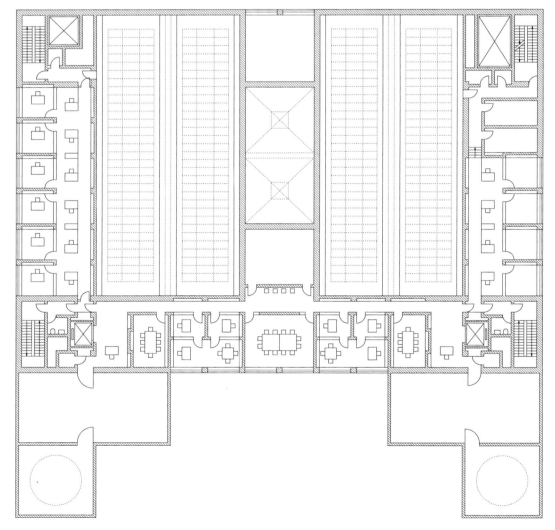

Fifth level

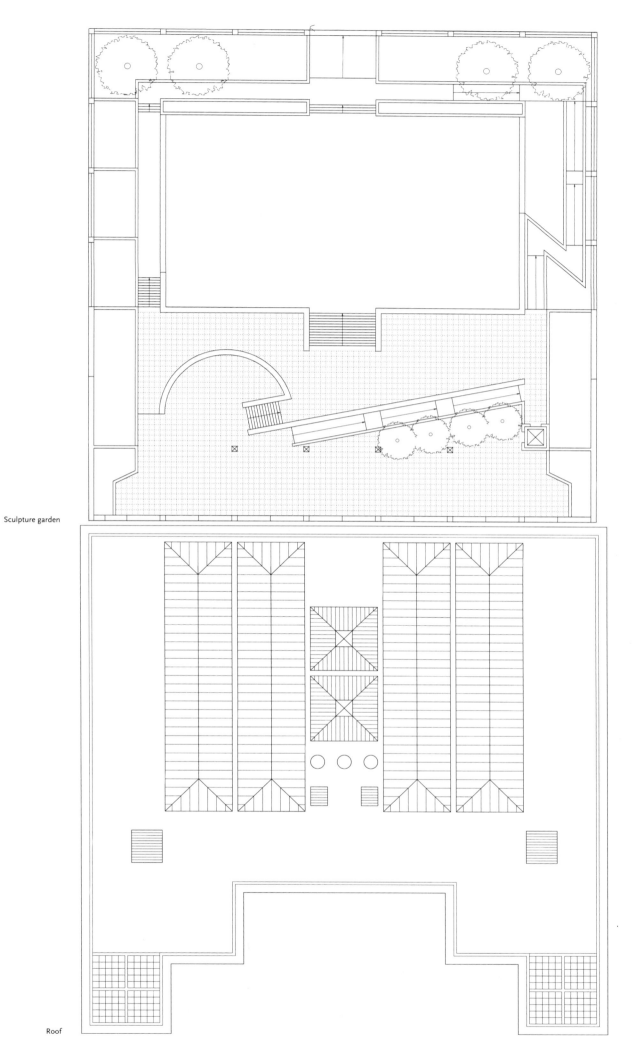

Sculpture garden

Roof

51

The sculpture garden

The sculpture garden is to the east of the museum and occupies the same square area as the museum building itself. It is reached from the museum level via the cafeteria and leads to a paved area that also serves the restaurant. The adjacent garden is terraced down to street level. The exhibition areas for the sculptures are arranged in various geometrical shapes and with the access paths they represent the design elements of a free composition. The arrangement respects the ground plan of the museum building in that a clearly perceptible central axis remains, leading from the central access to the garden to the gate at the rear. A diagonally placed ramp runs along the central axis, which obstructs the direct path between the entrance to the building and the garden gate. For this reason, from the lower level the view towards the museum is of a concrete wall that frames the ramp laterally and serves as a neutral background for the sculptures. The rational principle of a short path system is kept in mind by axial visual relation, while in fact use of the paths is governed by various steps and ramps.

The principle of interlinking rationally and poetically determined parameters that characterizes the architecture of the museum building is materially illustrated by the layout of the sculpture garden. It can at the same time be seen as a poetical co-relative to the museum building.

A straight ramp leads to the top terrace. The concluding wall provides a neutral background for sculpture.

The various levels of the stone terrace with free-standing walls offer a wide range of exhibition possibilities for sculpture.

East façade.

The form and texture of the concrete walls contrast with the geometrical surface of the building´s rear façade.

Elevations

The façade structure of the five-storey building is divided into three in the classical tectonic pattern: base, wall zone and cornice. This is not so much an allusion to the historical motif, as the clarity is legitimized by the functional articulation of the building. The main entrance to the museum is on the second floor, while the first floor provides access to facilities that are not directly related to exhibition matters. The entrances cut into the corners of the building to the bookshop in Chicago Avenue or to the lecture theatre and Education Center in Pearson Street are specially accentuated and count as fundamental access elements. Like the central entrance, they too have a combination of revolving and wing doors. Cutting under the body of the building at the same time produces a roofed entrance that is sheltered from the wind.

The clearly protruding roof cornice and the strong shadow that it casts give the effect of an upper conclusion to the building. In this way the completeness of the building in all directions, including upwards, is emphasized and attention is drawn to its autonomous character within the particular urban situation, in which it is placed as an art refuge. The bordering experience invoked by the Propylaea motif of the steps is thus accentuated by the sense of completeness exuded to the outside world - and art is emphasized in this sense as a sphere that distances itself from that world. But once visitors are inside the building they have precisely the opposite experience in terms of transparency and openness: art offers itself as an alternative to what already exists and in this way claims social significance for itself.

Entrance façade cut-out.

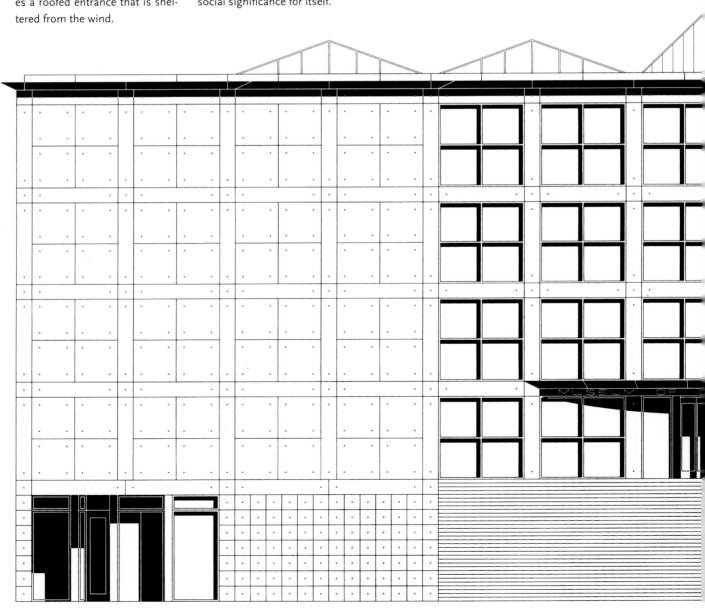

Complete view of the
museum from the west.

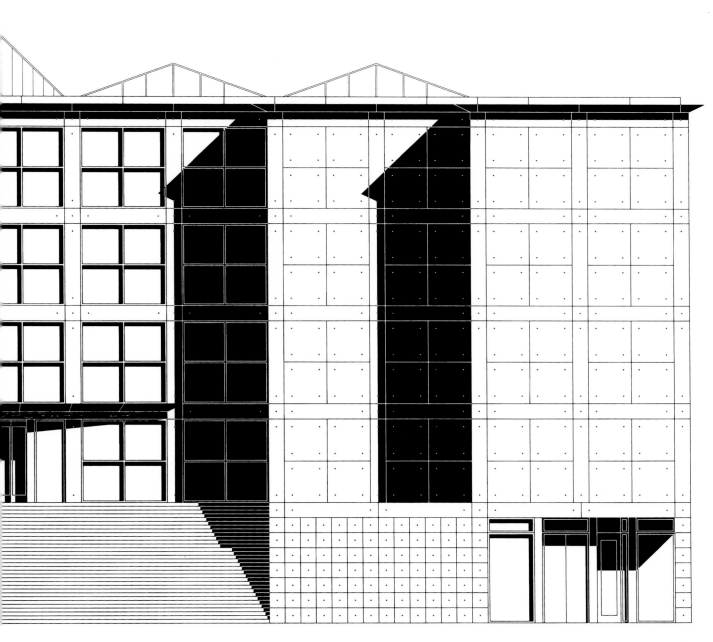

Plasticity and large
wall areas combine
to produce a mo-
ment of architectural
repose in a busy
urban landscape.

The broad entrance steps are an invitation to linger. The negative development of the building above the base zone creates a sculpture pedestal.

The iron banister of the entrance steps rest on shipshape connecting pieces.

On the entrance façade the building block is set back in two vertical steps from outside towards the centre. This produces a 26-foot deep, square sculpture pedestal above the base on each side of the 16-foot staircase, which rises from the outline edge of the building. The staircase's further thrust towards the glazed core area makes this shift backwards in a second phase, so that an overall effect of the façade receding in steps is produced. The articulation of the façade is based on the square constructional grid that is in evidence to the outside in the size and arrangement of the cladding elements.

Limestone cladding in the staircase area.

The side façades are characterized by large, continuous wall areas, broken by individual windows
both in the wall zone and the base
storey in accordance with the functional arrangement of the offices
and classrooms. The placing of
the windows in the base storey –
where the emergency doors are
also situated – demonstrates particularly clearly how the ideal geometry has been shifted. It is quite
clear that they do not relate to the
axial dimension of the wall zone
and therefore do not always correspond to the run of its joints.

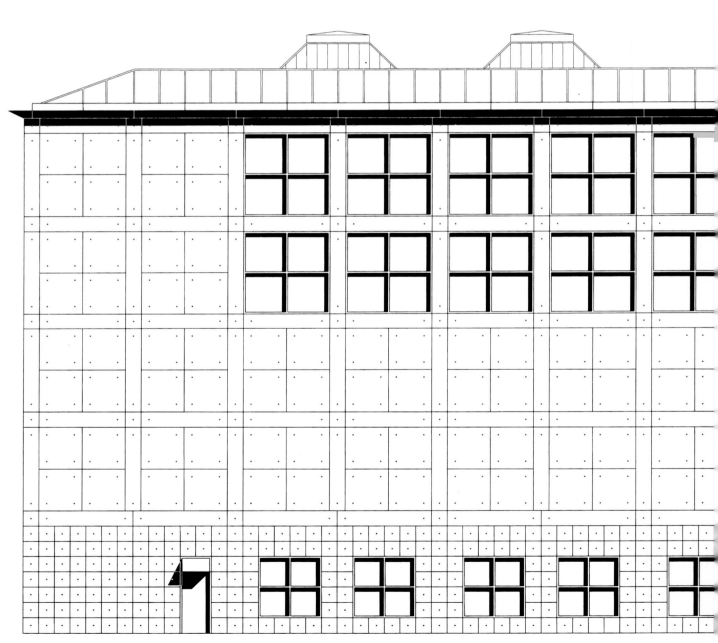

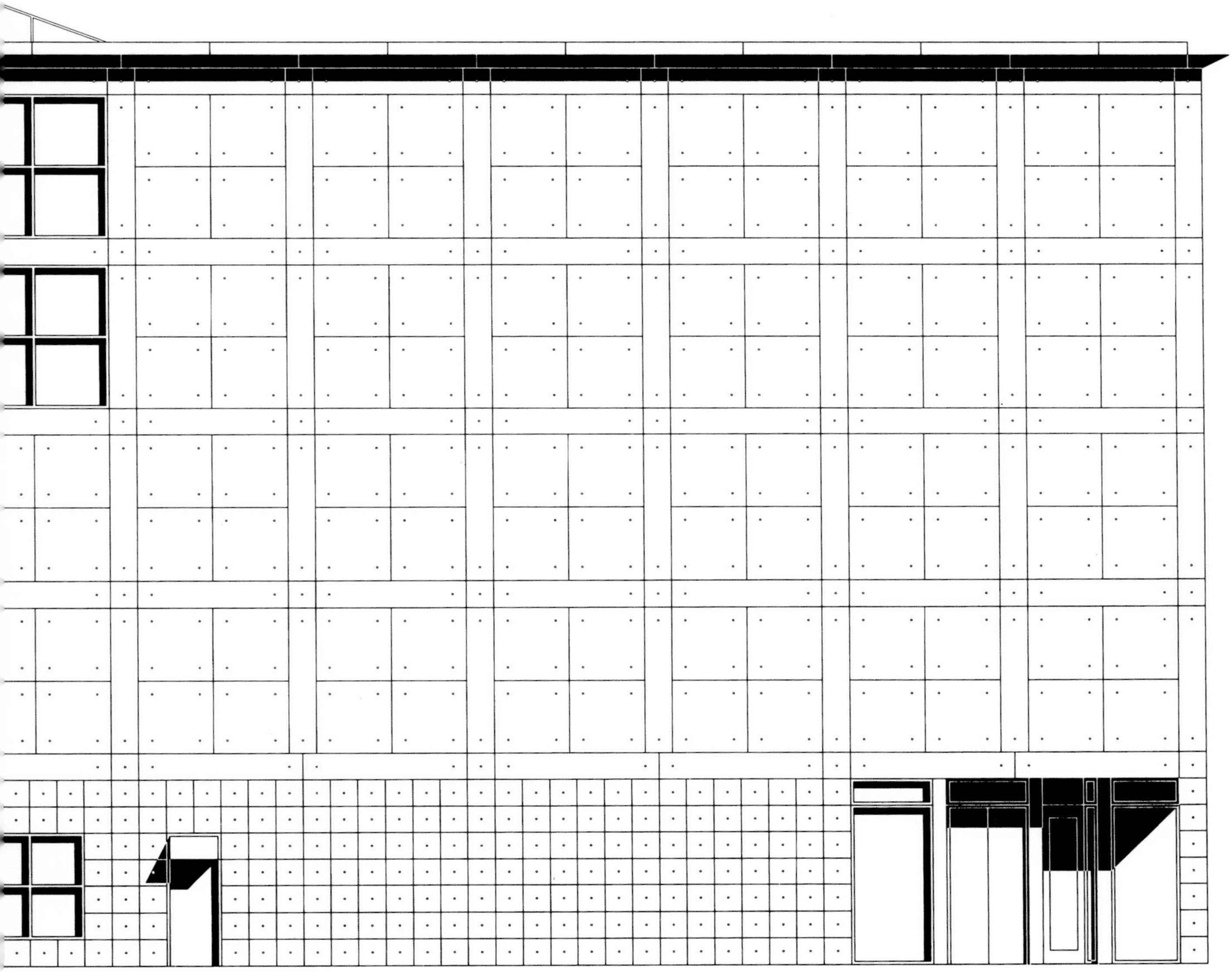

The window arrangement on the rear façade of the MCA shows the spatial disposition of the cafeteria and the atrium. The base storey is missing here, as the sculpture garden is directly connected with the first exhibition level on the second floor has an artificial incline under which the museum car park is placed. Instead the base storey, analogously with the sculpture garden continues as a side border with gridded iron railings and finally marks the boundary of the museum area on the eastern side with an open view from the outside. The basic form of the double square of museum and garden is thus revealed, but remains visually permeable.

Façade detail with aluminium cladding.

View from Chicago
Avenue over the rail-
ings that frame the
garden to the rear
façade of the building.

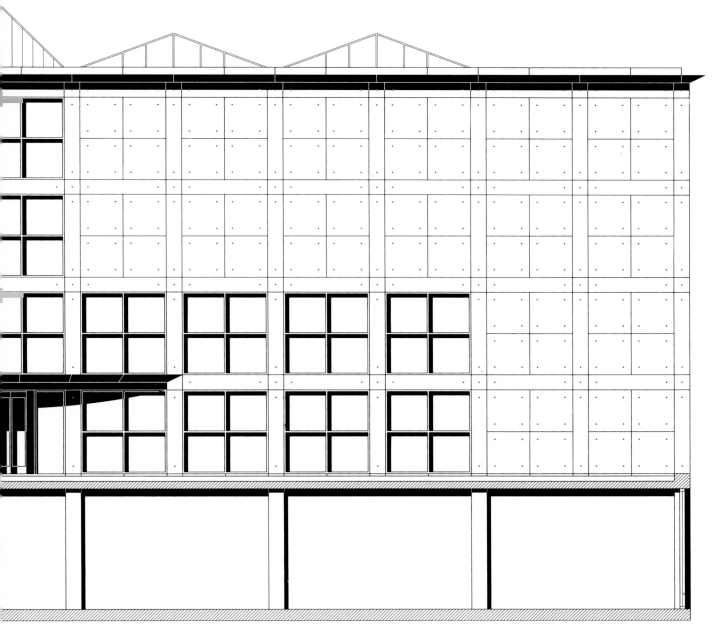

The Chicago Avenue
side façade of the
museum has charac-
teristically large wall
surfaces in which
individual window
incisions emphasize
the regularity of the
structural grid.

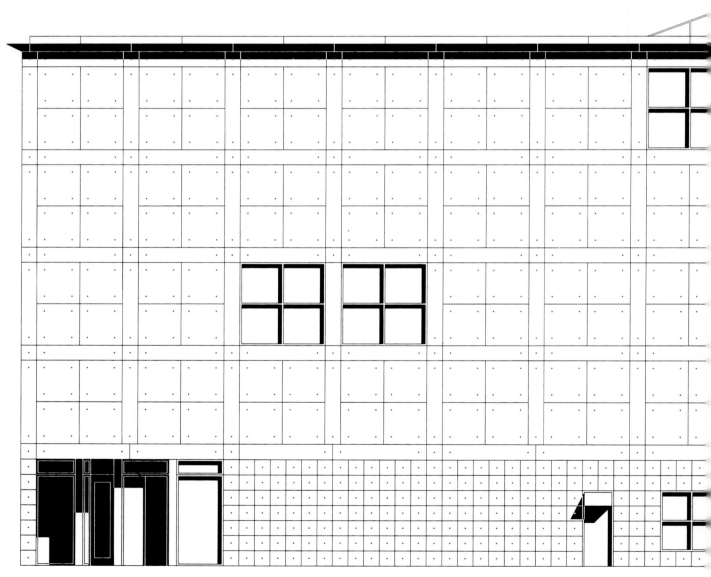

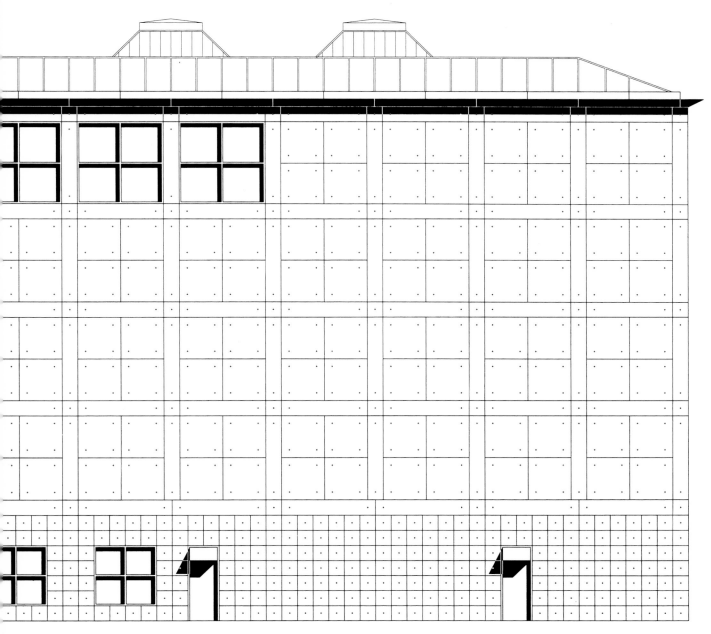

Roof installations

Josef P. Kleihues also looked carefully at the design of the roofscape when conceiving the building, as the new museum is surrounded on two sides by skyscrapers in its urban context, and thus particular attention had to be paid to the view of the building from above. This was taken into account in the design of the roof installations, like for example the intakes for the air-conditioning and by retracting technical apparatus into the interior of the building.

The roof installations were specially designed by Josef P. Kleihues as the Museum can also be seen from above in the gorge of buildings.

The pyramid roof of the atrium can be seen behind the steel roof installations.

Interiors

The motif of the cover and its development towards the interior is experienced by visitors in a striking way when they pass through the revolving doors of the main entrance into the inside of the museum. In contrast with the closed effect of the exterior, the main lobby, dominated by the white colour of the wall surfaces above a dark floor covering in Impala Black, creates breadth and transparency and uses natural light in a variety of ways. Josef P. Kleihues says: "I want this building to communicate simplicity, openness, quiet, as well as the interplay between transparency and containment, these are the key elements. It is also very important

The sculptural quality of the casement sections designed for the museum windows is revealed.

to create spaces for viewing art that allow viewers to be isolated with the art, to be separated from stairs or elevators. The visitor must be able to come to a dialogue with the work of art, without distraction."

Spatial hierarchy is imposed by size, disposition and the communicative relation of the spaces to each other. So the transversely placed lobby extends through two storeys and across the breadth of the glass façade on both sides. Straight ahead it leads into a central atrium that includes all floors and is additionally lit vertically by large square skylights. If the restaurant and cafeteria are included in this open spatial concept, this produces a double T-profile ground plan.

The multidimensional breadth of the lobby is an invitation to linger and to get one's bearings in the building. The view on both sides leads to the lifts and the stairs beside them – going down to the bookshop on the right and on the left as a link with the other museum floors – while the view through the atrium runs through the cafeteria with the glazed rear façade and leads to the sculpture garden and then on to Lake Michigan.

A glass door divides the cafeteria from the atrium.

Shadow-play

Visitors can discern the vertical and horizontal penetration of the space from the foyer.

View in the opposite
direction.

Lighting strips are integrated into the walls of the atrium, running round the edge of the ceiling. An impression that the space is opening upwards is created, which might legitimately be seen as reminiscent of the floating concrete roof of Le Corbusier's chapel in Ronchamps in eastern France. The viewer's reception runs counter to the conventional perception of the support structure, thus subtly supporting the transparency of the overall spatial impression.

Le Corbusier, Notre-Dame-du-Haut chapel, Ronchamp, 1950-55. Light penetrates from outside through the slit below the concrete roof, thus giving an impression of lightness.

Lateral relations.

At certain times of day, light is concentrated by the skylight.

Pyramid roof skylights above the atrium.

The continuous lighting strip running round the shoulder of the roof increases the impression of transparency and lightness.

The spatial effect of the atrium is determined by various direction-values.

The core elements, with access on the right and left of the atrium, on this main level are two exhibition galleries on a square ground plan with sides 76 feet long. These spaces are for temporary exhibitions and are conceived without supports, with a view to the greatest possible flexibility using mobile screens. The building grid of 26 feet or its subdivisions is visible in the structure of the ceiling lighting, which covers the whole area and corresponds to the image of the cast aluminium façade. Light scatter is guaranteed by the use of translucent glass panes.

Vertical and horizontal grid.

The atrium provides
many relations for
the eye between the
various levels.

The white paint deter-
mines the impression
made by the light-
flooded atrium.

The galleries for tem-
porary exhibitions are
furnished as plainly as
possible to give
maximum flexibility.

The museum steps.
Dissolving the ship-
shape form on various
landing levels causes
diverse breaks in the
step structure.

The diagonally aligned staircase
by the north lift connects all the exhibition levels and the Education
Center lobby. It is in the form of a
shipshape and as a white-painted
steel structure with Impala Black
steps is reminiscent in passing if
the interior steps in the Rookery in
the Loop (Burnham & Root, 1885-
86). Through the eye of the staircase there is a view of a pool of
water with a bench beside it at the
foot of the stairs, which is related
as a motif to the similar arrangement that Frank Lloyd Wright used
in the Solomon R. Guggenheim
Museum in New York. The staircase leads up to the video-gallery
on the third floor, a mezzanine
floor, and to a balcony in front of the
lifts with a view of the main lobby.

The iron staircase in shipshape form links up all the museum levels.

View from below of
the iron construction
with stone covering.

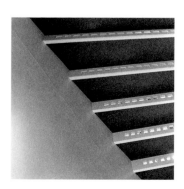

The view up the stair
well to the skylight
shows the complex
iron structure with
Impala Black stone
covering.

View downstairs.

Frank Lloyd Wright,
Salomon R. Guggen-
heim Museum, New
York 1956-59 (1943
Plan). The shipshape
fountain in the Main
Gallery and the ship-
shape staircase in the
side building can be
made out in the
ground plan.

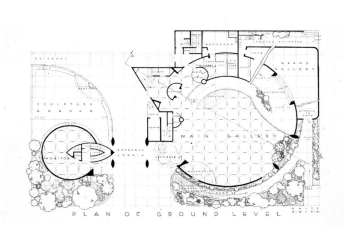

Guggenheim
Museum, fountain

The foyer preceding the galleries for the permanent collection invites visitors to linger and offers a view of the run of Chicago Avenue.

Upper foyer. The lift can be seen in the background.

The museum area ends on the fourth floor. On this level there is a second foyer over the entrance hall with a connection to the lifts opposite, a kind of gallery with a view of the city and – on the other side – down into the atrium. This gives access to the longitudinally aligned galleries for the permanent collection. Here visitors are able, in contrast with the rooms on the ground floor, to make a round tour of the exhibition, in the course of which they have another look down into the atrium or outside into the sculpture garden from another gallery on the building's rear façade.

View into the atrium
and a side gallery
from the upper foyer.

The window frames the
urban corridor between
the Water Tower and
the Museum.

This view into one of the northern exhibition galleries and the adjacent atrium shows the possibility of a circular tour of the upper storey.

Before the translucent glass panes are fitted the barrel vaulting shows the daylight regulation mechanism.

Two parallel
exhibition galleries.

The parallel naves of the exhibition
galleries are lit throughout their
full length by skylights whose natural incident light is dispersed by a
barrel-vaulted false ceiling in translucent glass and can be regulated
by a slat system.

The fifth floor, a mezzanine floor,
is limited to the front part of the
building. It houses various side-
rooms, the museum employees'
offices and a conference room.

The point at which the vault springs is marked by a shoulder.

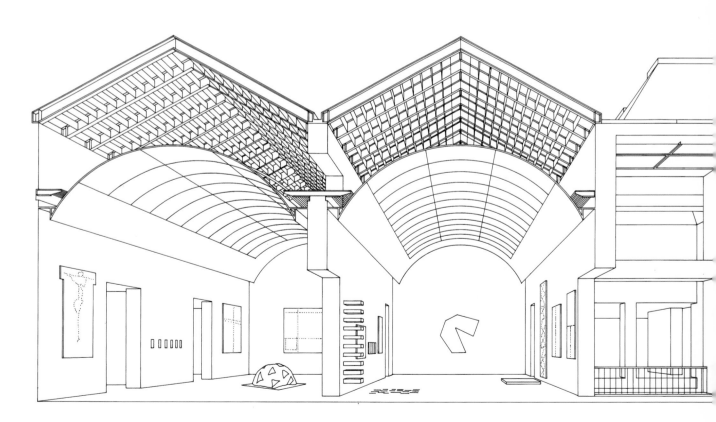

The barrel-vaulted galleries for the permanent collection are defined from above by a relationship of natural and artificial light that can be regulated.

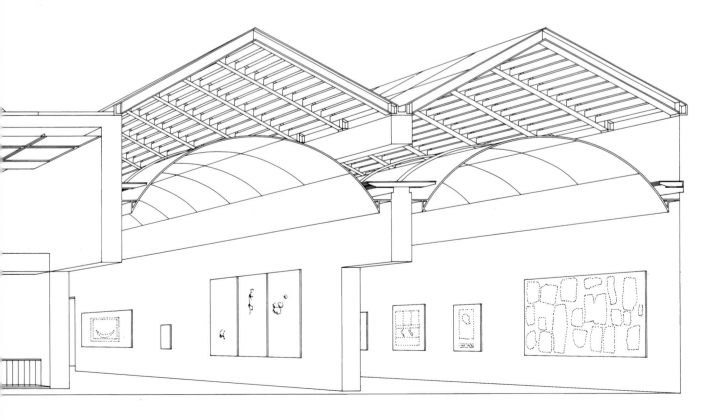

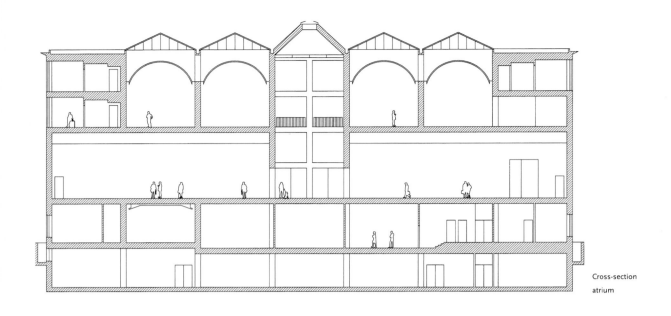

Cross-section
atrium

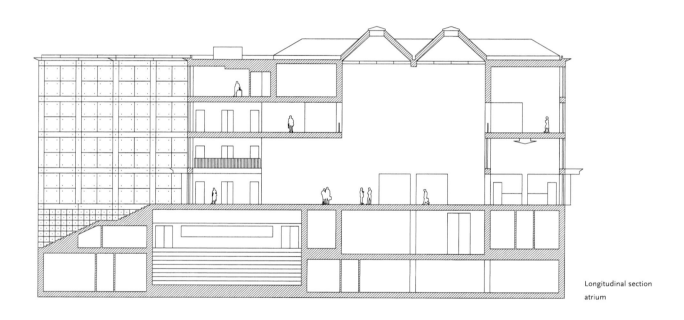

Longitudinal section
atrium

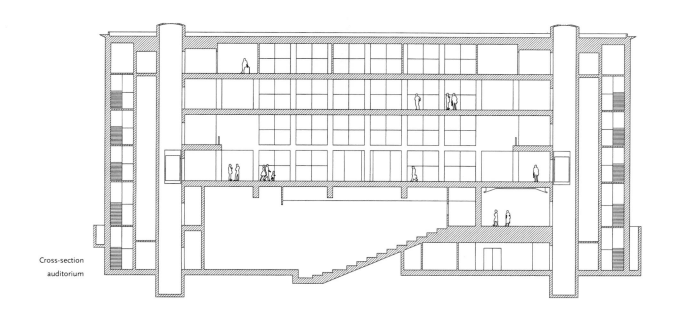

Cross-section
auditorium

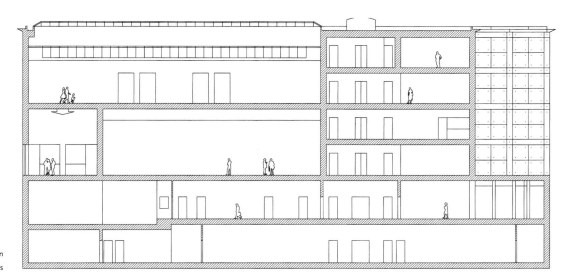

Longitudinal section
floor levels

A wood-clad shipshape
staircase combines the
two levels of the
bookshop.

The entrance level is directly connected with the bookshop via the right-hand side of the lobby; its selling areas can be opened completely independently of museum activities. The shipshape staircase that links the upper sales floor with the bookshop area on the first floor is a mirror image of the steel staircase on the north side, but it serves only the bookshop and in a spirit of making a unified impression with the fittings of the shop is in American oak. Kleihues designed the fittings, and they use large areas of this wood from

The rounded sales shelves in the bookshop surrounded by the square floor grid show the departure from the ideal geometry of the building´s ground plan on the ground floor.

which the doors, door-frames and handrails in the museum are also made. The shipshape motif is repeated in the sales counter, which is placed in a spatial extension of the ground floor under the sculpture pedestal on the façade side. The building grid is illustrated on the parquet floor by continuous bands of Impala Black.

The detail in the upper staircase base in the bookshop shows how the rounded shape meets the floor grid.

Square supports from the junction points in the bookshop´s floor grid of wooden covering and Impala Black.

Henri Labrouste (1801-1875), vestibule of Ste Geneviève by the Panthéon in Paris (1838-50).

Ground level access to the bookshop is by revolving door set diagonally in the visible gap in the
façade in the right-hand corner of
the building. The corner on the
left-hand side is treated in the
same way. It provides museum
access for the disabled, with a
spacious foyer leading to the lift,
the shipshape steel staircase and
the meeting room for the museum trustees, the Education Center
and the lecture theatre.

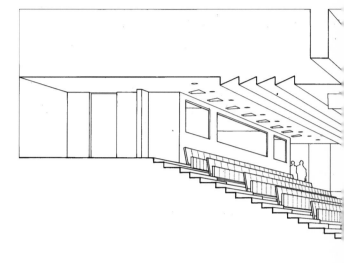

The Robert B. and Beatrice C. Mayer Education Center takes up a large part of the north side of the first floor. All the classrooms are naturally lit as they are arranged along the outer wall. The interior corridor is separated from them only by a glass screen. The lecture theatre seats 250 and is intended for film showings, performances and theatre presentations, as well as lectures. The auditorium ceiling is clad, for acoustic purposes and also to accommodate lighting elements. This also applies to the wood-panelled walls, which additionally have technical facilities for sound transmission as well as lighting. Visitors with walking difficulties are taken by lift to a podium between the rows of spectators.

Josef P. Kleihues has pointed out the pragmatic nature of the transverse placing of the theatre. In contrast with idealistic architectural concepts of European provenance, which suggest placing elements symmetrically to an axis, the MCA theatre is placed as a response to functional requirements: the two entrances to the lecture theatre had to be as near as possible to the north side entrance, so that the theatre could be used independently of the museum's opening times.

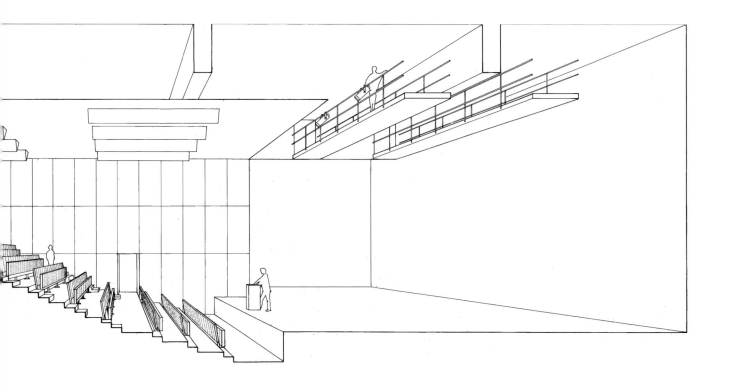

Materials

The tectonic structure of the building is shown by the change of materials between base and wall zone. The base is characterized by Indiana limestone slabs, in elements of 2 by 2 feet. In terms of colour, the use of this natural stone creates a link with the neighbouring historic Water Tower and Pumping Station.

The stones are 4 inches thick, and do not rest on bracket anchors, but were laid traditionally and are self-supporting, giving the impression of a solid base. But stable fixing (to prevent the wall from toppling over) is achieved by the use of countersunk screws, which are demonstratively placed in the centre of each slab. As a motif, the screw fixing is an allusion to Otto Wagner's Postsparkasse in Vienna (1904-06). Kleihues had already addressed the subject of cladding buildings in this way on several occasions, for instance in the Museum für Vor- und Frühgeschichte (pre- and early history) in Frankfurt (1979) or the Kantdreieck office building in Berlin (1984-94). But compared with the solution

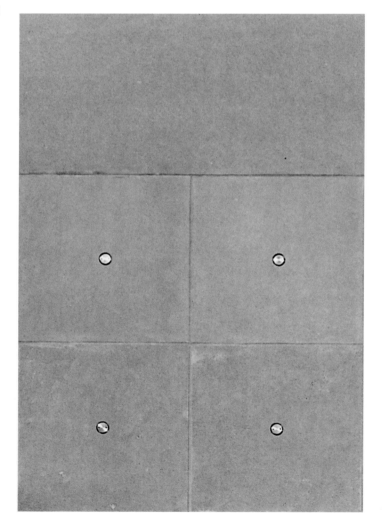

Indiana Limestone slabs with demonstratively placed screws.

he used for the "Kantdreieck", the pointing of the slabs in the MCA shows a significant difference. In both cases the screws are intended to express the fact that the material is cladding, the impression of solid masonry given by the pointing works against the transparency of the principle and makes the fixing screws seem merely ornamental. Here Kleihues is ironizing the problems of constructional truth posed by modern technologies.

Cladding for the wall zone above the limestone base was originally to be lead sheets 1 inch thick. But lead is not hard enough to meet the demands in the intended size, and its toxic qualities were also cause for concern. Instead of this, Kleihues decided to use wall elements made of cast aluminium, which could age like the stones of the base and would in time carry a distinctive and lively patina. The final processing of the finely structured aluminium sheets at their place of manufacture, El Paso, was by sandblasting with fine iron filings, which left tiny particles in the softer aluminium. Under the influence of Chicago's damp climate these particles have changed the colour shade and provided an early patina, a process that is still not complete. Independently of this unintentional process, Kleihues took the particular light conditions in the Chicago Avenue urban canyon into account. In view

of the extreme weather effects, this light means that the material presence of the different materials capable of ageing is made particularly clear.

In contrast with the cast aluminium façade elements the aluminium casement sections developed specially for the MCA were drawn polished and anodized in natural colours. The window formats and their division correspond with the constructional building grid and the ordering of other dimensions that in turn correspond with this. For the side façades this means leaving square fields blank appropriately to the use conditions of classrooms and offices. On the entrance façade the core area is glazed to the full height of the building, and this glass is divided into square areas by aluminium bands running at right angles to each other and thus also integrated into the grid structure of the rest of the façade. The same is true of the rear façade facing the sculpture garden, which is glazed in the shape of a "T" standing on its head, corresponding to the breadth of the cafeteria and the height of the atrium.

Transparency and reflection are two qualities of glass that are as significant for the visual unity of the building as for its integration into the urban situation. The glass façade acquires double significance especially in terms of visual relations with the neighbouring buildings reflected in the glass and with nature. At night, when the surface becomes like a shining lamp, the sculptural quality of the building withdraws to its innermost parts. The receding core area of the MCA then seems to be extended into the interior of the building by a further dimension.

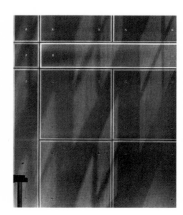

Detail of the aluminium façade with grid articulation.

Detail of joint between
aluminium cladding
and casement section.

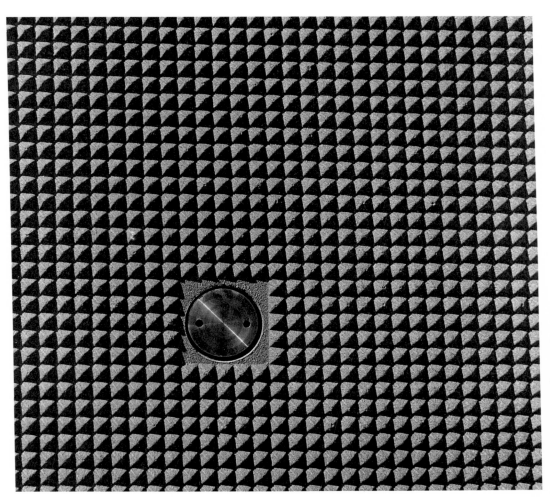

The aluminium
cladding elements
are fastened to the
external walls with
countersunk screws.

97

Windows

As in earlier projects, Josef P. Kleihues developed a system of casement sections for the MCA. This was used both for windows glazing and for the elements of the outside doors. These sections can be combined appropriately to requirements. They are in drawn aluminium, and their natural colour emphasizes the different processes involved when they are compared with the cast aluminium wall elements. The window sections in the base area emphasize the thickness of the material in the limestone walls cladding the base of the building and enter into a tense relationship with them.

The curves and edges of the window sections create a play of light and shade and enhance the lively effect of the façades in the changing daylight.

Axonometric
impression of the
square, fixed-
glazed 11 x 11-foot
window elements

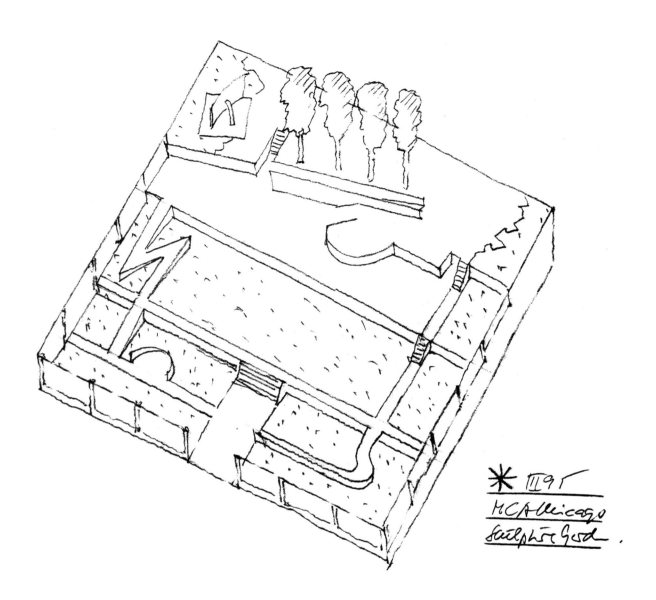

✳ III 95
MCA Chicago
Sculpture Grd.

The Architect Josef Paul Kleihues

Josef P. Kleihues in conversation in his Chicago office.

Josef P. Kleihues was born in 1933 in West-phalia/Germany. He studied in Stuttgart from 1955-57, from 1957-59 in Berlin under Peter Poelzig and Hans Scharoun and in 1960 at the École des Beaux-Arts in Paris. From late 1960 to 1968 he was project director for the Westend Head Clinic for Peter Poelzig's office, and parallel with this he founded his own office with Heinrich Moldenschardt in 1962, a partnership that was to last until 1967. From 1973 he held the chair of architecture at the University of Dortmund, where he organized the "Dortmunder Architekturtage" in the mid seventies, and as part of this architecture exhibitions involving international architects that attracted a great deal of attention. From 1968 to 1991 he was visiting professor at the Cooper Union (Irwin S. Chanin School of Architecture) in New York and in 1987 at Yale University, alongside his teaching activities in Dortmund. In autumn 1994 he left the University of Dortmund to teach architecture at the Düsseldorf Kunstakademie.

In the sixties Kleihues's own architecture was restricted to Berlin at first, where he realized his first outstanding project in 1969, the main workshop for the Berlin Municipal Cleansing Department. The unusual solution shows an analysis of more general architectural themes as well as logical fulfilment of function. It is typical of Kleihues's basic aesthetic attitude here that he understands the purpose of the building as well as the concrete task it presents.

In the case of the Cleansing Department this understanding shows as an architectural theme in linear accumulation by the repetition of basic elements. This theoretical reflection on the "principle of accumulation in architecture" was then documented under the same title in 1975 in the course of the "Dortmunder Architekturtage" Kleihues had initiated.

In 1973 Josef P. Kleihues submitted a successful entry for an invited competition to build the hospital in Neukölln in Berlin. The design takes the aesthetic possibilities of stringent modular order as a general architectural principle as its subject. To an extent this presents a problem in terms of the tradition of rationalistic architecture, as the design expresses neither the industrial and economic aspects of rationalization nor the simplifying schematism of an abstract will for order, but reflects on an aesthetic understood to have already become historical that Kleihues places in a general historico-theoretical context.

The residential development on the basis of a 1972 design in Block 270 in Vinetaplatz in Berlin-Wedding represents an important statement on urban development questions. The principle of block-edge development, which was being heatedly discussed at the time, is treated as a problem with a long tradition in Berlin history. In this, as in all this architect's projects, architectural and urban development

questions are inseparably linked and complement each other mutually. The intensive involvement in urban development that grew out of the architectural concept led in 1979 to his work as planning director of the "Internationale Bauausstellung" (International Building Exhibition), which was to be momentous for both him and Berlin. He was a major influence on urban development discussion there from then on. In the period of the exhibition to 1987 Josef P. Kleihues exercised restraint as far as his activity in Berlin was concerned. Apart from the residential building "Haus an der Brandwand", which was realized in Schöneberger Straße, which shows the interlinking of urban ground plan and building ground plan that is typical of his work, Kleihues realized no large buildings in Berlin but restricted himself to a series of projects in West Germany and completion of the hospital in Berlin-Neukölln.

As well as this field of work, which also made Kleihues internationally known, his reputation outside Germany is based not least on his intensive involvement in museum buildings. Kleihues had addressed a large variety of architectural tasks, and used them to question the architectural and theoretical principles of his work; nevertheless museum building appears in numerous examples as a kind of project that was tackled on a particularly large number of occasions. Particular attention was drawn to this fact in 1989 by an exhibition about Josef P. Kleihues's museum projects in the Arthur A. Houghton Jr. Gallery at the Cooper Union in New York, which introduced him to the American public.

Some works should be mentioned as examples here that show the architect's approach to tackling museums in very different ways. First the Museum für Vor- und Frühgeschichte (pre- and early history), Frankfurt am Main 1980 (building work to 1989). One condition imposed on this new building by the clients was that an existing building, a former Carmelite monastery, should be incorporated; it was one of the few surviving medieval buildings in Frankfurt. Kleihues's solution places a third bar parallel to the two existing, long monastery buildings that are to be retained and restored. His building, through which the transepts of the church cut, concludes the museum area as an alley running along the plot, and houses the main entrance to the museum. This creates a courtyard situation between the new building and the choir of the church, which Kleihues accentuates with a glazed extension and which accommodates a cafeteria.

This coming to terms with existing historical development, which is made particularly vivid because the parts of the building interpenetrate, can be seen as typical of Kleihues's procedure of allowing the *genius loci* of a place to make its mark in his designs. As well as the arrangement of the buildings, the use of certain materials typical of the place (in this case red Main sandstone) should be mentioned as a means of relating to the urban situation. This does not curry favour with the historic substance, but creates a striking connection with what is already there,

Main workshop for the Berlin Municipal Cleansing Department, 1969-75.

Block 270 in Vinetaplatz, 1971-76.

while the architectural form identifies the new building as autonomous architecture. The cladding of the façade of the new building on Alte Mainzer Gasse, together with the fact that the stone slabs are fixed with stainless screws, shows a striking similarity with the MCA, where Kleihues again returns to this theme. Kleihues had already used this motif of fastening the façade cladding with screws for the Henninger Museum and the Städtische Galerie Kornwestheim in 1987, and it has been repeated on many of his buildings since. Historically it relates to the example of Otto Wagner's Postsparkasse in Vienna (1904-06).

Kleihues's design for the conversion of the "Hamburger Bahnhof" for the Museum für zeitgenössische Kunst (contemporary art) in Berlin was completed in parallel with the MCA in Chicago. This is a extension to the historic railway station, which ceased to function as such in the 19th century; it is planned as a building with two wings. The historic stock was converted into exhibition galleries and for other functions. Kleihues used the opportunity of being able to build museums in Europe and America at the same time to create a number of links between the MCA and the "Hamburger Bahnhof", in this way creating a correspondence across the distance between them. Thus the designs can be seen to have various things in common. The conception of the long, tunnel-vaulted exhibition galleries, the staircase motif in the entrance area and the use of cast aluminium as material for the façade in particular should be mentioned here.

Alongside his perception of architecture as an interface for historical, philosophical and architectural-theoretical discourse, there are ways of looking at problems individual to the work of Josef P. Kleihues that appear in a dialectical relationship to these superordinate themes. They are pursued over long periods of time and make the level of insight clear at various points in the development of his work. Even the early work reflects a wish for rational justification of all parts of a structure in the spirit of constructional and structural transparency. This wish does not contradict the anticipation of something mysterious brought about by the poetic aspect of the designs, but on the contrary creates a special connection in their competitive relationship, which appears as a specific quality of experience in the work of Josef P. Kleihues.

Critical Reconstruction of the City

From 1979 to 1987 Josef P. Kleihues was planning director of the "Internationale Bauausstellung" (International Building Exhibition; IBA) in Berlin, and in this context he formulated his urban development concept of the "critical reconstruction of the city". The guiding idea for the "South Friedrichstadt" district as one of the central planning areas in the exhibition is fundamentally based on reflection on the lost 17th century urban structure in ruined Dorotheen- and Friedrichstadt. But Josef P. Kleihues stresses that the distortion or dissolution of the system of blocks of buildings based on the right-angled grid plan of the baroque city expansion was not just a consequence of the war. It was also affected by the division of the city, and by town planning that sanctioned this condition on both sides; south Friedrichstadt came under West Berlin's political jurisdiction. Kleihues's urban development concept was first developed in this inner city district that was so clearly defined in terms of Berlin's history, then later destroyed, but he later tried to make the concept more generally significant – in the new building district in the suburb of Tegel, for instance. Thus it is already becoming clear that in Kleihues's theoretical perception critical reconstruction is neither restricted to prescribed, historic urban structures nor to inner city districts. It can be applied to the various ordering principles of other cities with their own traditions and it aims at future-oriented urban design.

As a project with historical validity, critical reconstruction is based on a sophisticated judgement of the historical conditions of its present. Tradition and modernism appear as two dialectically related reference-points, and have to be considered by appropriately to their development. Thus the historical development principles of continuity, break and variation are perceived as competing modes of historical behaviour that have to be examined critically in terms of their present development. The aesthetic development principle of Modernism – here Modernism should be understood as the objective-functional architecture of the twenties, as developed in Germany in particular – was based on the idea of a progressive negation of traditional sense-links. Breaking through structures experienced as conventional is here seen as a critical gesture against conditions favouring prestige, economic exploitation and – generally – the confirmation of traditional social power relationships. But because Modernism always has to relate to the system from which it wishes to distance itself, the dialectical principle of Mod-

Museum für Vor- und Frühgeschichte (pre- and early history), 1980-89.

ernism can never completely detach itself from tradition. The historical principle of this procedure finds itself in an aporetic situation: on the one hand tradition as a whole can be criticized only through negation of its principles, on the other hand its structure determines the criticism. This process admits only an either-or in structural terms and thus cannot avoid aporia.

Modernism itself is therefore reduced to historicizing the aesthetic expression once produced, which can now realize itself only if previous criticism has

failed; this is supported by Theodor W. Adorno's notion of the "most advanced material" as a characteristic of modern art. Its validity lasts only as long as the duration of its advancedness. The possibility of criticism for the modern work of art therefore becomes dependent on the possibility of progressive negation of tradition. But once this negation is complete, the historical project of Modernism is in structural-theoretical danger. Kleihues's theory reacts to this situation by further developing the model on the basis of, and not by rejecting, modern principles, and by replacing either-or with both-and. He draws on Aldo Rossi's urban development theory (L' Architettura della Città, Padua/Italy 1966), in which architecture and urban development are considered together and, going against the modern idea (in the sense described above) of complete autonomy, respect for the historical ground plan is built in. Thus a theory emerges that expressly admits contradictions, contrasts and breaks, recognizing them in a spirit of intentional plurality. "For the conception of our work, the idea of critical reconstruction of the city is more open and takes more pleasure in experiment, in contrast with Rossi's reductive theory emphasizing relation to tradition. In the spirit of a totality that is not superficially harmonious, but diverse, we wanted and had to accept, contrasts and contradictions as aim and method." (Kleihues) Thus historic development of any urban structure is perceived in this sense as an accumulation of competing models, which have to be harmonized not by establishing unity, but by keeping their individual quality.

As in the case of Berlin it is not possible to establish an ideal image of the kind that has possibly shaped other large cities that have developed historically, Kleihues's conception aims at analysis of and consideration for the history of the individual places. The quality of the city should be promoted in a well-proportioned relationship of continuity and innovation, "by which it changes from its own order that was once created, while 'remaining the same'". The city appears in this formulation as the subject of change, the urban developer as the court of appeal that understands the city's urge to change on the basis of a responsible historical analysis as a parameter of its design practice.

The concept of the "inner city as a place to live" as an element of "critical reconstruction" corresponds to the desire for improvement of inner city residential quality and express emphasis on the necessity of mixing functions. Tackling problems of living in a city qualitatively is seen here as an important requirement for designing an individual and collective

Städtische Galerie Kornwestheim, 1987-89.

Museum of Contemporary Art Berlin "Hamburger Bahnhof", 1989-96 (under construction).

environment that is close to life. The plurality of various life forms requires diverse typological differentiation as a response.

Kleihues's negative attitude to the architecture of the 1957 International Building Exhibition (Interbau) was finally – rightly – transformed into a benevolent attitude, in a spirit of the required diversity. For Interbau a group of distinguished architects from the Modernist camp (like Alvar Aalto, Walter Gropius, Oscar Niemeyer) developed the war-damaged and totally refurbished Hansaviertel in Berlin, following the guideline of producing a "varied, greened city" without considering urban development relations; buildings were considered in isolation, as high-rise, terraced or detached houses with garden courtyards. However, many of these so very different building types and residential ground plans have

stood up so outstandingly well to the demands of an enormous variety of life situations that this model city embedded in a kind of park still remains a popular address.

The restriction, recently imposed in Germany, to use of the urban block and its historically developed scale is often misunderstood as authoritarian; this restriction is firstly more sophisticated in its intention, but even in the concretely realized urban space the antitotalitarian option of the concept has been confirmed. Kleihues is concerned to follow the idea of critical reconstruction and "use the building individualities that are required and impose their own requirements effectively as parts of a living urban order."

Diversity and unity appear here as complementary concepts. They cannot be separated from each other and even less can they be played off against each other. Diversity, if the concept is seen not as an abstract category but as a complex expression of an urban culture, cannot be experienced without unity. This banal statement, once the insight has been acquired, becomes an important regulatory protection against the physical and also the spiritual stripping to bits of the city. The irreducible claims of competing models which really are available in the city as

historical results can be experienced in the sense of urban development plurality only through the joint relation system.

The question of the intended function mixture in the sense of critical reconstruction virulent only through the block, which appears as a functionally differentiated spatial unit.

The simple urban structure of Dorotheenstadt (from 1674) and Friedrichstadt (from 1688, extended from 1713, south Friedrichstadt from 1732-38 to plans by Philipp Gerlach) goes back to comparable town expansions in 17th century Holland and even further to the system of streets intersecting at right angles named after town-builder Hippodamus of Miletus (5C BC). Unlike the typically baroque approach to the city gates (Brandenburger, Potsdamer, Hallesches Tor) and the squares associated with them, which help to unify the urban space visually, an unhierarchical structure comparable with the 1609 expansion of Amsterdam was preferred for Dorotheenstadt and Friedrichstadt. A grid structure of this kind proved its worth above all for newly-founded American cities, after being introduced by the Spanish in the 16th century and systematized for the United States by Thomas Jefferson in 1785. As the cities grew rapidly in the 19th century, closed block-edge development emerged from this. "The building block represents ... something like a microcosm of the city, a meshing of functional and formal diversity." (Kleihues)

The 19th century Berlin Hobrecht Plan (1862) produced a building block whose closed and stereotypical form was broken up only for special uses. Critical reconstruction of the building block is definitely to be perceived as criticism of this monotonous structure. It poses problems in a way that relates to a tradition within Modernism itself by aiming to enrich the living space. In the mean time, a break with the building block structure was tried out on various examples even in the late 19th century as a protest against the social evils of the tenement blocks. These experiments aimed "to respect the historical ground plan of the city", as Kleihues emphatically points out, while loosening up the block structure. In the twenties a definite break was made when the important peripheral estates using the terrace method appeared, without abandoning the concept of development on the street periphery.

Further development of this concept for the inner-city area was prevented, and it was not taken any further under the pressure of rebuilding in the post-war period. Instead, most of the stock that the war had left standing was destroyed out of concern to meet the enormous need for housing.

Against the background of this context, critical reconstruction was intended to examine the building block and try experimental variations while respecting historical development. This strategy, between tradition and Modernism, seems a sensible way of trying out a third approach, which introduces the urban development parameter of extending aesthetic resources without ignoring history.

It is inadmissibly one-sided to suggest that Modernism never recognized diversity; but in a process of model construction that is still under way, diversity is becoming the general basic constitution as an extension of modern paradigms. For Kleihues it is conceptually anchored as an "effort to develop Modernism in a way that relates to history". Kleihues supports plurality from historical experience, not through negligence.

In this context, "experiment and risk" are expressly understood as essential components of Modernism. They have to be developed further and are brought into play as key concepts in resisting the diagnosed paralysis of "economic-technical-functional thinking". And this is the starting-point for another concept coined by Kleihues, that of "Poetic Rationalism".

Poetic Rationalism

In Josef P. Kleihues's concept the notion of poetry relates to the concept of rationalism dialectically. But "rationalism" is more a wide-ranging tradition than an object-area that can be precisely defined. With "Poetic Rationalism", Kleihues is resisting one-sidedness in architecture as a result of the twenties tradition of functionalism, in Germany in particular.

This kind of architecture is always reproached for its lack of "poetry" because of the functional and rational basis of its approach. This turned out to be artistically, and thus also socially disastrous, especially when it was radicalized in dubious further developments after the Second World War. Now functional rationality was also being criticized in other cultural spheres. Criticism of the traditional panel painting – clearly present in the diverse expressive forms of contemporary art – is to be seen in this context, for example, just as much as the long tradition of philosophical critiques of rationality since the Enlightenment. In this century it was probably formulated most powerfully and with the same tendency as Kleihues's approach by Theodor W. Adorno.

In about the mid sixties, Josef P. Kleihues distanced himself from his very personal, narrative design practice in order to bring a direct architecture characterized by clear geometrical principles to the fore. Rational criteria, which make the design comprehensible in all its elements, are approached "poetically" and enter into a "dialogue of contrasts". Kleihues's commitment to the demands of functionality, economy and series thus at the same time contains his critique of "instrumental rationality" and "naïve functionalism", which can both be traced back to the twenties' perception of rationalism. "Poetic Rationalism" is a drastic expansion of a rationalism that is interpreted only technically, functionally and economically: on the one hand we have the abstraction of geometry and on the other the concrete things and facts of the place and the task in hand with which the architect is confronted and for which he gains recognition in the design.

With a view to the autonomy of a building in the Modernist sense, Kleihues thus brings about a structural break that goes far beyond voluntary concessions to a certain aspect of the design. Kleihues does not want to get rid of or ignore things that are old, on the contrary, he works on the basis that his structures will co-exist with other buildings and thus detaches himself from the anti-traditionalist basic requirements of the "International Style", as this has now become historical itself.

This attitude requires a theoretical foundation, which Kleihues considers to be as binding and guiding for design practice as his constant examination and refinement. For him it includes political, philosophical and ethical ground rules as well as artistic principles, and thus forms a free set of rules that responds to the particular situation. Each of his designs is the result of an intellectual process in which the programme of use and the place are studied precisely and fused with the theoretical basis to produce a building idea that is only then put on paper. But cultural tradition and history lead to the *genius*

Hospital in Berlin-
Neukölln, 1973-86.

loci, not just the physical place; they open up the possibility of finding an individual, non-transferable architectural solution for the task in hand. Theoretical clarity and artistic quality give the building the necessary autonomy and create a handwriting for the architect's work that is common to all his buildings.

The starting-point for Kleihues's interpretation of rationalism is the rationalism of the Enlightenment. The French Academy of Architecture, founded by Colbert in the late 17th century, set up a very ambitious normative aesthetic, an *ordre général*, intended to restrict individual interpretation as much as possible, but dogmatic classicism started to be liberalized even in the 18th century. The characteristic feature of the new enlightened attitude was the sudden low valuation of aesthetic norms in favour of functional criteria in terms of building use and in relation to physical and urban conditions. From now on beauty was irrevocably linked with function and comfort, and the declared unity of the good, the true

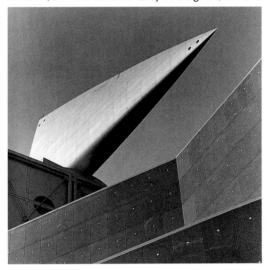

and the beautiful was interpreted as "the useful, the true and the beautiful", the germ of modern functionalism. Architecture was to become formally simple again, clear in its statements and characteristic in artistic expression. The laws of proportion were the objectifiable theoretical basis here.

The demands of the various tendencies towards enlightenment in 18th century classicism finally led to French "revolution architecture", although this was not politically "revolutionary", but revolutionary in its approach in terms of architectural theory; it helped an absolutely rational attitude of mind to an extremely vivid formal language. One of its main protagonists, Etienne-Louis Boullée (1728-99), first drew attention to the poetic component of architecture in his "Treatise on Art" by pointing out the impact buildings have on the viewer's emotional world. He therefore placed a particularly high value on the pictorial idea of a building, before practical scientific implementation. The development of German classicism was to a certain extent dependent on developments in France, even though it was less austerely rational. This was replaced by a much more rapid move towards eclecticism, which was thought to promise functional solutions, and histor-

icism in an anti-academic, Romantic interpretation. This move away from formalistic dogma was particularly expressed in Germany by the foundation of the Berlin Bauakademie in 1799. Here the greatest emphasis was placed on technical training, inclining to functionalism. Against this background Karl Friedrich Schinkel (1781-1841) developed a very comprehensive understanding of architecture, which offered a number of points of departure for development throughout the 20th century, where he was also perceived as paving the way for Modernism.

In the United States Thomas Jefferson (1743-1826) assumes the role of the first architectural theorist to appeal to the universal and, as he believed, democratic statement made by the formal language of antiquity; he campaigned for the adoption of architectural classicism as the national building style for the newly independent America. His "cubic architecture", reduced to basic geometrical forms, links Jefferson with the revolutionary French architects and make him one of the most radical and important representatives of American Palladianism. As an architect, Jefferson is to be blamed for the mistake of translating ancient forms literally into the New World and new functions, but it is to his credit as a theoretician that he recognized the universality of rational principles in classicism.

Josef P. Kleihues reacts to the demands of the Modern movement for functionality, economy and series with "Poetic Rationalism" without sentimentality, but by giving these ideas new validity and rationally extending them by adding abstract pictorial values and references in clarified form. Rational principles, not because of a higher order, but so that it is possible to use them as a basis for reflecting critically and objectively about what has always been there, using them as a basis. Thus the contradiction of rationalism and poetry is only apparent; it enables a lively exchange of reason and sensual experience in the design process or, in other words, makes it possible to experience the atmosphere of a place, atmosphere as "a mixture of spirituality and concrete life-rhythm". Sensual experience is not the irrational factor that flows subjectively into the design. Sensual experience is the component that is made graphic substantially and outwardly by the geometrical abstraction of the rational design: in construction, in material, in detail.

Detail that is carefully planned and executed also plays a part in this discussion about abstraction and graphic quality. As a mediator between intellectual design work and craftsmanlike manufacture, visible constructive detail gives the building a human scale in the social sense; the building becomes comprehensible and identifiable.

In the Museum of Contemporary Art the mingling of poetry and rationalism is complete: the impression made on the viewer by the body of the building, broken open on the entrance side, in its material and geometrical lucidity, in its transparency and solidity, is powerfully pictorial. The abstract principles are conveyed sensually and initiate a perception process that reveals the mysterious poetry of a spatial conception mingling with the *genius loci*. The interpenetration of interior and exterior that can be experienced through the glass façades on the entrance and garden sides corresponds with a continuation of the urban ground plan into the interior of the building. It thus suggests not so much a withdrawal into the "temple of the arts" as being placed, both physically and spiritually, in a historico-geographical and historico-cultural space. The experience of space that is possible in the museum as a result of diverse directions of view and movement emphasizes the universal dimension of time, one of the most penetrating motifs in the history of architectural theory. A high point within the complexity of this spatial structure conceived according to rational principles is the consummate gesture of the sculpture garden as a transition to the infinite breadth of Lake Michigan.

The lucidity of the freely composed sculpture garden certainly represents a qualitatively new element of the confrontation between poetry and rationality for Kleihues as well, but it would be a misunderstanding to try to limit the architectural realization of the theoretical concept to this point. Just as the design of the strictly rationalistic building is based on a "poetic" component, i.e. the inclusion of its effect – from which it is clear that the transverse placement of the lecture theatre cannot be seen as a "poetic" deviation from the design, it is in fact a purely pragmatic decision – the poetic element we perceive the sculpture garden to be is not merely ornamental. Etymologically, poetry contains an element of doing, and Kleihues alludes to this: "It is something that evolves through a specific activity and thereby leads to the authentic work." Poetry and rationalism are therefore not to be seen as counter-concepts; their relationship expresses a concrete view of rationality that associated rationality inseparably with the concept of "poetry".

This rationality derives not from the exclusively functional definition of the architectural design, but from its consistency in the historico-theoretical sense: it is aesthetically necessary. To this extent it is neither chance nor the result of a purely subjective decision by Josef P. Kleihues that the technicist, function-rational determination of architecture since the early seventies – especially in Germany – is being expressly criticized by him. Rational legitimation derives from the fact that he is consciously acting entirely appropriately to the historical development of the aesthetic material and the questions that this raises.

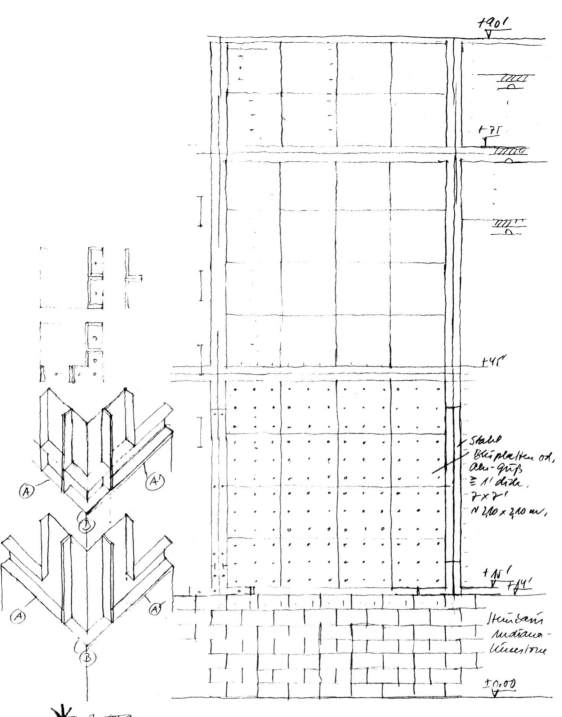

+90'

+75'

+45'

Stahl
Bleiplatten od.
alu-guß
≡ 1' dicke,
7 × 7'
N 210 × 210 m,

+ N'
+ 14'

Steinbau
indiana-
limestone

± 0,00

✳ 3. VIII 91
HCA Micago
M + K – Fanade,

Street canyon in
Chicago Avenue.

The square of the
sculpture garden is
made up of a lawn
and a paved terrace
in a free combination
of geometrical forms.

On the History of the New Building

The Museum of Contemporary Art in Chicago was opened by private initiatives on 24 October 1967 after a preparation period of three years. Its first home was a single-storey building at 237 East Ontario Street, and from here, after extending its space to three store, it gave considerable impetus to cultural life in Chicago with much-admired exhibitions of American and international art, by promoting Chicago art and thanks to its educational activities.

In the eighties the increasing size of the permanent collection and greater number of events gave rise to thoughts about the possibility of expanding, which led to a decision that a new building was needed. The National Guard Armory site on East Chicago Avenue was under consideration from 1986. In 1990 the State of Illinois made the Armory land available for 99 years for a symbolic rent of $1 per year. An international search was announced to find an architect for the new building. After a twelve month selection process German architect Josef P. Kleihues emerged as victor in May 1991; his designs for the new museum and sculpture garden were presented to the public on the occasion of the MCA's 25th anniversary on 19 March 1992. In spring 1993 the Armory was pulled down and excavations for the new building, which was financed by contributions, could begin. The opening ceremony took place on 21 June 1996.

A fundamental criterion for the handling of the selection process was the commission members' responsibility to the public, because it was accepted that Chicago had no architecturally significant museum at the time. The MCA was privately financed, and decisions were taken by the Board of Trustees jointly with the director of the museum. This led to the time-consuming conscientiousness devoted to the individual entries. There were over 200 submissions, of which about half came from the United States, and after several selection phases six very different architects were shortlisted. The architects were then interviewed, and visits were paid to their major works, and the finalists were invited to Chicago to discuss particular conceptual points on the spot.

Questions to Josef Paul Kleihues

During the selection procedure for the new museum, representatives of the Museum´s Board of Trustees questioned Josef P. Kleihues, himself a collector of contemporary art for many years, about his view of the public commission and how a contemporary art museum should present itself.

What are your thoughts on the role of contemporary art museums in society today?

The special role which will be played by the Museum of Contemporary Art cannot be understood in isolation from the role which museums in general play in today's society.

For some years increasing attention has been paid to the museum as a public institution with an ever broader range of programmes, demands and expectations. One reason for this attention is to be found in the sheer number of museum projects – ranging from the small to the outright spectacular – which have been carried out at home and abroad during the last twenty years. A further reason is to be found in the fact, that a large section of the public has an ever increasing amount of time to use for its leisure and education. There is a confusing variety of demands, however, which are placed on the museum as a "social" institution. There is talk about temples of fine arts, places where we learn about historical developments and social conditions, of environmental museums and of the museum as a field of action. Something to suit everybody.

But what seems to me to be making an important contribution towards the growing interest in museums as places where the most varied of items are collected and preserved, classified and presented, is a new public awareness of history that is determined not only by the intellect but also by the emotions. It is here that the concept and practice of recollection plays a key role. The concept of recollection, however, is as dependent on the relationship between reason and history as it is on the fundamental assumption that reason is freedom.

This is particularly true for a museum of contemporary art. It is in such a museum that the proximity of history to the present age is clearly perceptible.

It is precisely for this reason, that it is important for such a museum to maintain a balance between enlightenment and pure aesthetics. Instruction which has gone too far is as harmful to recollection as a celebration of art which eshews all words.

Recollection is a life-affirming opportunity for both unchanging and new perceptions. A museum can best fullfill the opportunity provided by recollection by presenting collections (whatever their subject) in a way which transmits something of there mystery and aura, thereby also allowing for a deeper intellectual and emotional knowledge of the individual objects.

What would be your design approach to an urban museum? How might you describe the museum's "street presence"?

The site for the Museum's new building is unique. The elongated piece of land between Michigan Avenue and Lake Michigan is akin to an artificial canyon in which the towering walls of the surrounding buildings represent a cross-section of Chicago's history.

Whenever the museum as an institution makes specific use of the concept of recollection (as defined above) for its work, it must also take care that this concept is apparent in the architectural-spatial quality of its building, for it is only through recollection that architecture and urban design can impart themselves in new variations.

We are convinced that the museum's "street presence" will be formed by its architectonic character. The nature of this presence depends on the manner in which it responds to the *genius loci*.

It is our conviction, that the individuality of a building (i.e. of a piece of architecture) should be a rendering of its purpose and of the "spirit of the area" in which it is located.

What are the strengths and weaknesses of the Armory site and the location of the new museum?

The special quality of the site — its relationship to open space — is rarely found in large cities. Its position between two green areas provides the museum with a number of possibilities. It could use this space as an expanded field of action, as an entrance (seen from Michigan Avenue) and as a museum garden with an unobstructed view of Lake Michigan. It would be difficult to find a location in Chicago which is better suited to the dialogue between transparency and safety which is so characteristic of an art museum.

Furthermore, the site's dimensions (especially its width of approximately 220 feet and its proportions of approximately 2:1) are particularly suitable for the museum's inner organization, above all with respect to its exhibition rooms and their lighting.

What are your thoughts on museum circulation, sequencing of galleries and the relationship between public and private spaces?

As the "client", it should be primarily the Museum's task to describe the new building's character, programme and functional spatial relationships. When a small group, consisting of some of the Museum's founders and trustees, has committed itself to the construction of a museum for contemporary art, one must assume, that they have quite clear ideas about the future building. These ideas should be incorporated into the design at an early stage.

The idea of having a permanently fixed arrangement of rooms in a museum of contemporary art is not a very appealing one. On the other hand, the idea of having rooms in a museum which can be constantly changed has also shown itself to be of little practical use. A concept should be developed, therefore, which guarantees that there will be an arrangement of rooms suitable for exhibitions but which over longer periods of time would also allow for changes required by individual collections and exhibitions. The technical and constructional prerequisites for this should be planned in such a way that the effort and expense involved could be kept firmly under control.

What are your views of gallery lighting?

This is a controversial subject and can never be resolved in purely objective terms. For this reason, the following comments should be understood as an aid to orientation. On a more detailed level, they permit for refinements and modifications.

Natural lighting for the exhibition rooms (with the obvious exception of those used for drawings and prints) should be one of the design's primary aims. The design should also guarantee, however, that it is not only "cold", "grey" north light which falls into these rooms but rather should provide for a wealth of light with all spectral colours. If this is not done, the objects (particularly the paintings) will be as dead as mutton. On the other hand, glare and greenhouse effects, as well as the irritating sound of automatically powered sunscreens are to be avoided.

Describe your typical design process from beginning to end.

Experience has shown, that the course taken by the design process is very dependent upon the client's programme, requirements and active participation. Nevertheless, it is necessary to differentiate between the methodological, organizational procedure and the course taken by the analytic and creative work on the design.

The analytic and creative work on the design is actually not a long process. As a rule it is usually a short, decision-making phase during which the programme and location are analysed and the image of a geometrically functioning order is developed. The design is then refined and improved as the work progresses.

Client

Museum of Contemporary Art
Museum Director and Chief Executive Officer:
Kevin E. Consey
Project Manager: Richard Tellinghuisen

Design Review and Building Committee:
J. Paul Beitler (Chair), Edward F. Anixter, Richard
H. Cooper, Gerald S. Elliott, Helyn D. Goldenberg,
Marshall M. Holleb, John C. Kern, Lewis Manilow,
Mrs. Robert B. Mayer, Robert N. Mayer, Dr. Paul
Sternberg, Jerome H. Stone, James R. Thompson,
Allen M. Turner, John Vinci

Architect Selection Committee:
Allen M. Turner (Chair), Mrs. Edwin A. Bergman,
Kevin E. Consey, Mrs. Thomas H. Dittmer, Joan W.
Harris, Ada Louise Huxtable, Bill Lacy, Robert N.
Mayer, Paul Oliver-Hoffmann, Jerome H. Stone,
Gene Summers, and Richard Tellinghuisen,

Architect

Josef P. Kleihues
Project Manager: Johannes Rath
Project Team: Greg Sherlock and Mark Bastian,
John DeSalvo, Pablo Diaz, Arden Freeman, Haukur
Hardason, Richard McLoughlin

Associate Architect/Engineers: A. Epstein and
Sons Int'l., Inc.
Executive Vice President: Michael Damore
Project Manager: Mark Streetz

Consultants

Design Engineer: Ove Arup & Partners
Program Manager: Schal Bovis, Inc.
Lighting: Claude R. Engle
Security: Steven Keller and Associates, Inc.
Schiff & Associates, Inc.
Landscape: Daniel Weinbach & Partners, Ltd.

General Contractor

W.E. O'Neil Construction Company
President: Michael Faron
Project Manager: Jim Sikich

Illustration Sources

Hélène Binet: 14b, 15, 40, 43, 44, 45, 46a, 48, 50a, 52, 53, 54a, 55a, 56, 57, 60a, 61a, 62a, 64, 65, 68, 69, 70, 71, 72, 73, 74, 75, 76, 78, 79, 80, 81a, 82, 83, 84, 84a, 85a, 88, 89a, 89m, 89bl, 94, 95, 96, 97, 103, 104a, 107, 110, 116, 117, 118, 119, 120, 121, 122, 123, 124, 126
Andreas Löhlein: 104b
Archives Josef P. Kleihues: 8, 10, 12b, 17, 42m+b, 46b, 47, 49, 50b, 51, 54b, 58, 59b, 62b, 84b, 86, 87, 91, 92, 99, 100, 102, 103, 105, 109
Stefan Koppelkamm: 106
Archives Dep. History of Architecture, Dortmund University: 13b, 14m
Chicago Historical Society: 18, 20, 21, 22, 23, 24, 25, 26, 27, 42a
Thorsten Scheer: 28, 32a, 33, 37a, 101
S.P.A.D.E.M.: 70a

Willmuth Arenhövel/Rolf Bothe (ed.), Das Brandenburger Tor 1791-1991, Berlin 1991: 13ml
Carl W. Condit, The Chicago School of Architecture, Chicago 1964: 30al, 31a, 32b
Global Architecture No. 36, Tokyo 1975: 79b
Josef P. Kleihues (ed.), 750 Jahre Architektur und Städtebau in Berlin, Stuttgart 1987: 12m, 13m
Peter Murray, Renaissance (Weltgeschichte der Architektur), Stuttgart 1989: 30r
Dietrich Neumann, Die Wolkenkratzer kommen, Braunschweig/Wiesbaden 1995: 30b, 36b
Hermann G. Pundt, Schinkels Berlin, Ffm./Berl./Wien 1981: 13a
P. Saddy, Henri Labrouste architecte 1801-1875, Paris 1967: 89br
David Spaeth, Mies van der Rohe, Stuttgart 1986: 34, 36m, 36a, 37b, 38
Frank Lloyd Wright Monograph 1887-1901, vol. 1, Tokyo 1986: 12a
Frank Lloyd Wright Monograph 1942-1950, vol. 7, Tokyo 1988: 79m
John Zukowsky (ed.), Chicago Architecture 1872-1922, München 1987: 31b